ACTIVE LEARNING

STARS & PLANETS

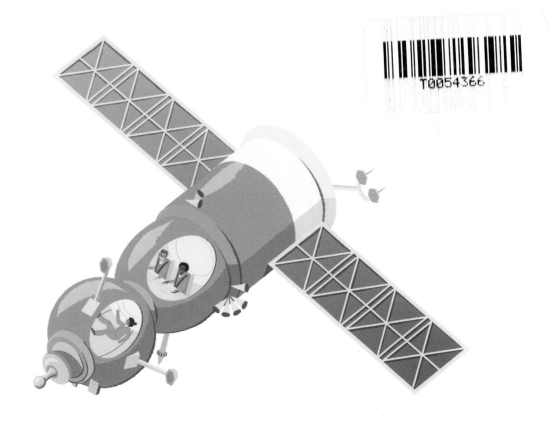

Penguin Random House

Senior Editors Catharine Robertson,
Rebecca Fry, Satu Hämeenaho-Fox
Editor Sarah Carpenter
Senior US Editor Kayla Dugger
Executive US Editor Lori Cates Hand
Senior Designer Phil Gamble
Project Art Editor Jessica Tapolcai
Managing Editor Carine Tracanelli
Managing Art Editor Anna Hall
Jacket Designer Stephanie Cheng Hui Tan
Jacket Design Development Manager
Sophia MTT
Senior Jackets Coordinator
Priyanka Sharma Saddi
Production Editor Gill Reid
Senior Production Controller Poppy David
Art Director Karen Self
Publisher Andrew Macintyre
Publishing Director Jonathan Metcalf

Illustrator Phil Gamble

First American Edition, 2023
Published in the United States by DK Publishing
1745 Broadway, 20th Floor, New York, NY 10019

A catalog record for this book
is available from the Library of Congress.
ISBN 978-0-7440-5615-0

Printed and bound in China

For the curious
www.dk.com

MIX
Paper | Supporting
responsible forestry
FSC™ C018179

This book was made with Forest
Stewardship Council™ certified
paper—one small step in DK's
commitment to a sustainable future.
For more information go to
www.dk.com/our-green-pledge

THE AUTHOR AND CONSULTANT

Lizzie Munsey writes and edits books for children. She has worked in publishing for more than a decade and has contributed to scores of books on a wide range of subjects, including space, science, natural history, geography, history, and math. Her favorite planet is Mars. Lizzie lives in Gloucestershire, England, with her two children, two cats, and a varying number of chickens.

Dr. Mike Goldsmith has a doctorate in astrophysics from the University of Keele, where he studied cosmic dust and supergiant stars. He has written more than 20 children's books about astronomy. Mike's work with DK includes titles such as *Amazing Space Q&A* and *Train Your Brain to Be a Math Genius*. He is a fellow of the Royal Astronomical Society.

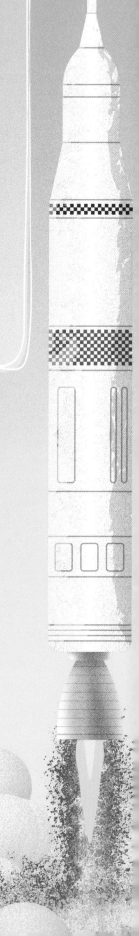

CONTENTS

CHECK WHEN COMPLETED!

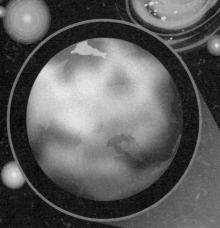

Earth
Our planet is one of eight planets in our Solar System.

One planet in space
The vast scale of the universe can be hard to understand. Here's how we fit in, on our planet, orbiting the Sun, in just one of the universe's many galaxies.

WHERE ARE WE?

The universe is enormous—it contains everything there is, including planets, stars, and colossal expanses of empty space. It has no center and no edges and is growing bigger. Earth is just one tiny part of the universe. It is one planet among hundreds of billions of others.

Solar System
Our Solar System is a group of planets that orbit a star—the Sun.

COMPLETE THE SET
The information on the cards has been jumbled up. Draw lines to put each card back together with a picture, a heading, and a description.

MATCH IT!

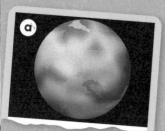 a.

 b.

 c.

 d.

SOLAR SYSTEM

EARTH

UNIVERSE

MILKY WAY

A galaxy that contains many stars, including the Sun

A vast expanse that contains everything there is

The planet we live on

The Sun and the group of planets that orbit it

```
M Z K F J
P Y W D G E A
Y U N I V E R S E
I V P E H T R A E N L
S O L A R S Y S T E M
O Y A W Y K L I M A K
R Z N F D L R G O L M
K E J P N L S R N
T Y X A L A G
N G G F P
```

FIND THE WORDS

Can you find the space-themed words hidden in this word search?

Earth   Universe   Galaxy

Planet   Solar System   Milky Way

DRAW THE UNIVERSE

Look at the universe across these two pages—it contains lots of galaxies, many of which have new stars forming within them. Use your imagination to complete the universe. Try drawing the galaxies first, then fill in the dark background at the end.

DRAW IT!

Universe
The universe is huge, and humans have explored just a fraction of it. There is so much more out there to be discovered.

Galaxy
A galaxy is a group of stars. Our galaxy, the Milky Way, has billions of stars, many with their own system of planets.

OUR SOLAR SYSTEM

A group of planets that orbit the same star (or stars) is called a planetary system. Our system is called the Solar System, because our star is the Sun ("solar" means "of the Sun"). The Sun is orbited by eight planets, some of which are orbited by their own moons. The Solar System also contains asteroids, dwarf planets, and icy balls of dust called comets.

MAIN ASTEROID BELT

THE SUN

MERCURY

VENUS

EARTH

MARS

The four planets nearest to the Sun—including our home planet, Earth—are made mostly of rock.

ROCKY PLANETS

COMPLETE THE PLANET-DOKU
Fill in this grid by drawing the Sun and planets. They should appear only once in each row, once in each column, and once in each box of nine squares.

Key

 The Sun   Mercury   Venus

 Earth   Mars   Jupiter

 Saturn   Uranus   Neptune

BONUS QUESTION
What word from Latin means a thing that is related to the Sun?

....

Orbiting the Sun
The four planets closest to the Sun are smaller and rocky. After them comes the Main Asteroid Belt—an area that contains tens of thousands of space rocks too small to be planets. The four planets outside this belt are larger and formed mainly from gas or icy liquids—they don't have solid surfaces.

THE EARTH COULD FIT INSIDE THE SUN 1.3 MILLION TIMES.

JUPITER

SATURN

URANUS

NEPTUNE

The four planets farther away from the Sun are larger balls of gas or ice.

GIANT PLANETS

WHICH PLANET IS WHICH?
Use the information from the image above to help you complete these planet fact files. Write the name of the correct planet from the box next to each letter. Read the clues carefully to make sure you don't get any of the planets mixed up!

Saturn   Mercury   Neptune   Venus

Earth   Jupiter   Mars   Uranus

WRITE IT!

a ....
The surface of this planet is red in color due to the red-colored iron oxide in its rocks.

b ....
This giant, blue ice planet spins on its side and has rings that loop around it from top to bottom.

c ....
The famous rings around this gas giant are made of rock and ice. It has low density and could float in water.

d ....
Our home planet is the only place in the Solar System known to have oceans of liquid water on the surface.

e ....
The closest planet to the Sun has very hot days and very cold nights. It is airless and has no atmosphere.

f ....
This is the biggest planet in the Solar System and the first outside the Main Asteroid Belt.

g ....
The farthest planet from the Sun, this ice giant looks blue because of the gases in its atmosphere.

h ....
Thick gases blanket the surface of this planet, which sits between Mercury and Earth.

The Sun's anatomy

The inside of the Sun is split into layers. Vast amounts of energy are created by nuclear reactions in the Sun's core, where the temperature can reach 27 million°F (15 million°C). This energy then makes its way up through the layers before escaping into space.

1 Core
The core is the center of the Sun. Nuclear reactions take place here, and these release energy.

2 Radiative zone
After the core is the radiative zone. Here, light energy slowly makes its way up and out of the Sun.

3 Convective zone
In this zone, pockets of gas expand and rise outward. Light energy moves faster here than in the radiative zone.

4 Photosphere
The thin layer of the photosphere is the part of the Sun we can see from Earth.

5 Sunspots
These cooler patches on the photosphere are darker than the areas around them.

6 Prominences
Long loops of gas can be thrown out from the photosphere. These are called prominences.

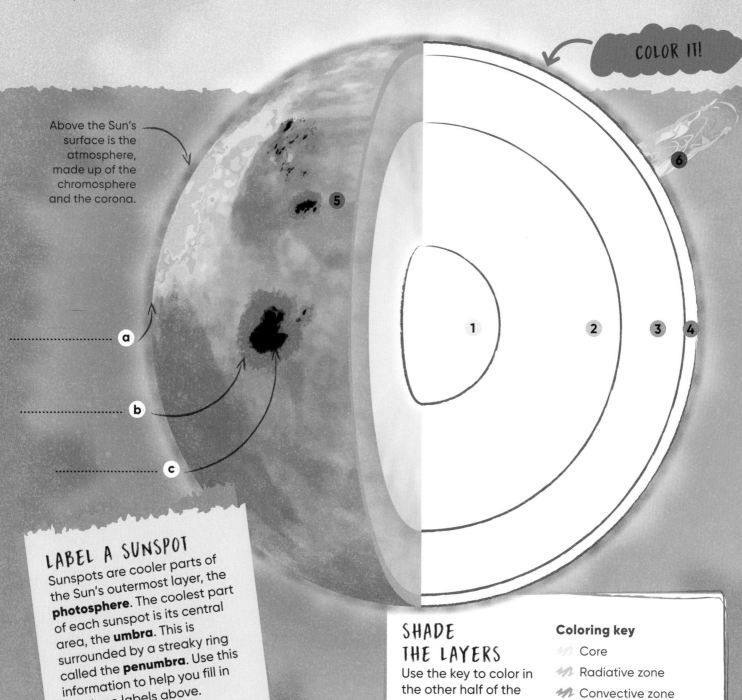

COLOR IT!

Above the Sun's surface is the atmosphere, made up of the chromosphere and the corona.

a ....

b ....

c ....

LABEL A SUNSPOT

Sunspots are cooler parts of the Sun's outermost layer, the **photosphere**. The coolest part of each sunspot is its central area, the **umbra**. This is surrounded by a streaky ring called the **penumbra**. Use this information to help you fill in the three labels above.

SHADE THE LAYERS

Use the key to color in the other half of the Sun's layers above.

Coloring key
- Core
- Radiative zone
- Convective zone
- Photosphere

THE SUN

The Sun is a star—a glowing ball of superheated gas that generates a huge amount of heat and light energy. It is the central object in our Solar System, and its gravity holds the Solar System together, preventing the planets from disappearing into interstellar space. Its pull is due to mass—the Sun is 330,000 times more massive than Earth.

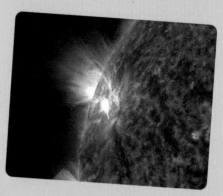

Solar flares
Solar flares appear as bright flashes exploding out from the surface of the Sun.

MATCH THE STEPS

The Sun rotates, but because it isn't solid, different parts of its surface rotate at different speeds. This affects the magnetic field lines running between its north and south poles. Over time, they get more twisted until loops break through the surface, creating sunspots. Eventually, the field lines snap, releasing bursts of magnetic energy called solar flares. Can you match these images to the correct stages in the process?

MATCH IT!

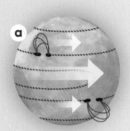
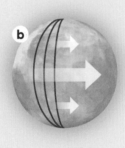

1 Spinning
The Sun rotates but at a faster speed at its equator (an imaginary line around its middle).

2 Twisting
The different spin rates mean the Sun's magnetic field lines become twisted.

3 Flaring
"Loops" of field lines poke through the surface and snap, causing bursts of radiation (solar flares).

START HERE!

FINISH HERE!

COMPLETE THE WORD SNAKE

Can you finish this word snake? It includes five parts of the Sun's anatomy. The first word has been started for you, and the other words run on afterward. Hint: you can move up, down, and across but not diagonally.

AURORAS

From time to time, dazzling displays of bright, swirling light brighten the skies around Earth's north and south poles. These light displays are called auroras. They occur when wind from the Sun hits our atmosphere at high speed, creating colorful curtains of light that seem to float in the sky.

ASTRONAUTS ARE ABLE TO SEE AURORAS FROM SPACE.

MATCH IT!

WHICH SHAPE?
Auroras come in many different shapes. Here are three forms they can take. Match each image to the correct description and write the answer below the picture.

a ....

b ....

c ....

Curtain
Wide stretches of light blanket the sky.

Crown
Rays appear to spread out from a central point.

Bands
Simple arcs of light stretch across the sky.

FIND THE AURORAS
These two auroras are all mixed up. They are at the wrong poles, and the letters are upside down and back to front! Can you unjumble them?

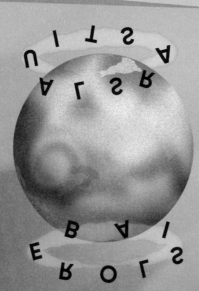

Aurora _ _ _ _ _ _ _
at the North Pole

Aurora _ _ _ _ _ _ _ _
at the South Pole

What causes auroras?

Auroras form when electrically charged particles in the solar wind collide with gas particles in Earth's atmosphere. We see them most at Earth's north and south poles, because our planet's magnetic field deflects some of the solar wind, directing it toward the poles.

Aurora borealis at the North Pole

EARTH

THE SUN

EARTH'S MAGNETIC FIELD

SOLAR WIND

Aurora australis at the South Pole

DESIGN AN AURORA

Auroras are usually green, but they can also be blue, red, pink, and yellow. Use the images on the left to help you complete your own aurora over this polar landscape below.

DRAW IT!

AURORAS CAN LAST FOR ANYTHING FROM A FEW MINUTES UP TO **SEVERAL HOURS.**

ROCKY PLANETS AND GIANT PLANETS

The planets in our Solar System are divided into two groups: smaller, rocky planets and giant planets. There are also two types of giant planets ("gas giants" and "ice giants") with different structures. Rocky planets orbit the Sun inside the Main Asteroid Belt and giant planets outside.

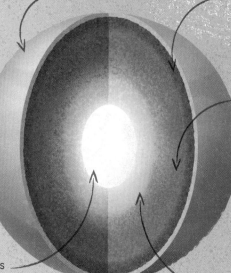

The **atmosphere** is one or more layers of gases that may protect, heat, or cool the surface.

The **crust** is a shell of solid rock.

The **mantle** is a thick layer of semi-molten rock that can slowly move around.

The **inner core** is a solid mixture of the metals iron and nickel.

The **outer core** is liquid metal.

Rocky planets

The rocky planets all have similar layers of rock and metals, though their size and exact components vary between planets. This diagram shows the inside of Venus.

THE GIANT PLANETS DON'T HAVE SOLID SURFACES, SO SPACECRAFTS CAN'T LAND ON THEM.

WHICH IS WHICH?

Read the descriptions of these planets to help you work out if each one is a rocky planet or a giant planet. Then check off your answer under each planet.

CHECK IT!

MERCURY

For its small size, Mercury has a large core, made of molten iron surrounded by layers of rock.

☐ Rocky planet ☐ Giant planet

SATURN

Saturn has a metallic core surrounded by liquid hydrogen and a deep layer of gases.

☐ Rocky planet ☐ Giant planet

EARTH

Earth has a solid iron and nickel core surrounded by molten rock. Its surface is solid rock.

☐ Rocky planet ☐ Giant planet

NEPTUNE

Neptune's solid core is buried beneath hot liquids, and it has a thick layer of atmospheric gases.

☐ Rocky planet ☐ Giant planet

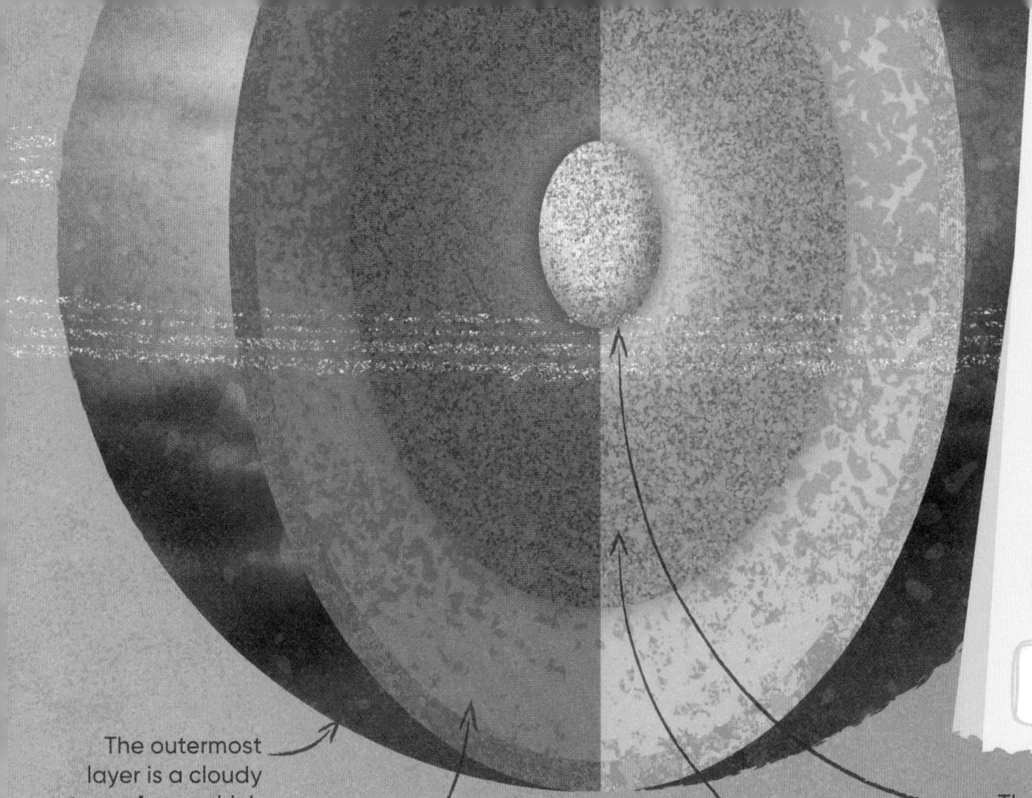

The outermost layer is a cloudy **atmosphere**, which contains a mixture of chemicals.

Beneath the cloud layer is a layer of **liquid hydrogen.**

Giant planets

These are made mostly of a mix of gases (gas giants) or liquids (ice giants), with a small rocky core. This diagram shows the inside of the gas giant Jupiter.

There is likely to be a small, solid **core** of rock and metal.

Outside Jupiter's core is a thick layer of **liquid metallic hydrogen.**

UNSCRAMBLE THE NAME

What is the name for the layer of gases that occurs around a planet? Unscramble the letters around this planet to find out.

P H A S T E M R
O H A S T E M E

_ _ _ _ _ _ _ _ _ _

SPLIT THEM UP

These giant planets, rocky planets, and asteroids have become jumbled up. Can you draw three straight lines to sort them into sections, each with one giant planet, one rocky planet, and one asteroid?

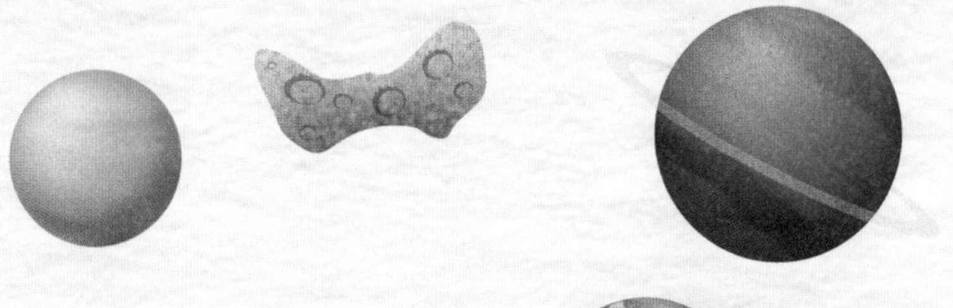

SORT IT!

13

MERCURY

The planet closest to the Sun is Mercury. It is small, rocky, and extremely hot, with surface temperatures reaching 800°F (430°C). Mercury moves around the Sun faster than any of the other planets, which is why it was named after an ancient Roman god with wings on his heels.

MERCURY
SPINS
ON ITS AXIS
VERY SLOWLY
COMPARED TO THE OTHER PLANETS.

The planet Mercury
Mercury is a mixture of rock and metal, with a solid surface. The planet has little atmosphere to protect it, which means even tiny meteorites crash into the surface, leaving it marked with craters.

Craters show where the planet has been hit by meteorites.

The atmosphere is thin, because Mercury has low gravity and is constantly blasted by the Sun's heat.

MATCH IT!

MATCH THE FEATURES
Mercury's surface has been shaped by the impact of meteorites over billions of years. Read the descriptions of Mercury's surface features below, then draw lines to connect each one with the correct image.

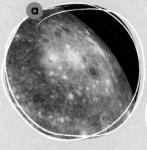
a

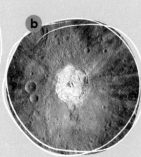
b

c

Kuiper Crater
The streaks radiating out from this crater show where surface material exploded during a meteorite's impact.

Plains
Huge plains show where lava once flowed. They are pitted with small craters, where more recent meteorites impacted.

Caloris Basin
This massive crater is one of the biggest in the Solar System. The yellow area was covered by lava after a meteorite impact.

COMPLETE THE MISSIONS
Mercury is so close to the Sun that spacecrafts must avoid our star's strong gravity, as well as the intense heat. The cards on the right show the three spacecrafts that have visited Mercury so far. Read the facts in the box below and use them to fill in the blanks.

To send two spacecrafts together to Mercury

2004

Took the first photos of Mercury's surface

TEMPERATURES ON MERCURY GET **SO HIGH,** THEY COULD **MELT LEAD.**

COLOR THE MAP

Temperatures on Mercury are extremely hot in the areas facing the Sun but extremely cold away from it. At night, temperatures can be as low as –275°F (–170°C). Use the colors in the key to complete this temperature map.

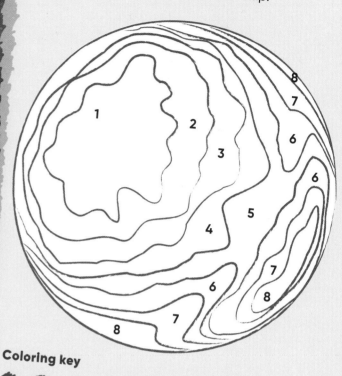

Coloring key

1 2 3 4 5 6 7 8

Hottest areas   Coldest areas

MERCURY

Average diameter: 3,032 miles (4,879 km)

Average distance from Sun: 0.4 AU
1 Astronomical Unit = 93 million miles (150 million km)

Year: 88 Earth days

Day: 176 Earth days

Moons: 0

MARINER 10

YEAR OF LAUNCH:
1973

AIM:
To orbit the Sun, studying Mercury on its way past

KEY ACHIEVEMENT:

BEPICOLOMBO

YEAR OF LAUNCH:
2018

AIM:

KEY ACHIEVEMENT:
Unknown—mission is still in progress

MESSENGER

YEAR OF LAUNCH:

AIM:
To orbit Mercury itself and study the planet

KEY ACHIEVEMENT:
Mapped all of Mercury

VENUS

This rocky planet is the second from the Sun, orbiting between Mercury and Earth. It is slightly smaller than Earth and spins very slowly in the opposite direction to most of the other planets. Venus is the hottest planet in the Solar System and is covered in thick, yellowish clouds.

The planet Venus
Although Venus and Earth are both molten inside, their surfaces are very different. Venus has the thickest atmosphere of all of the rocky planets and is covered in sulfuric acid clouds.

THE **FIRST PROBE** TO VENUS'S SURFACE SURVIVED FOR JUST **1 HOUR** DUE TO THE INTENSE **PRESSURE & HEAT.**

The surface
Volcanoes dot the surface of the planet. Some are likely to be active and adding more sulfur to the atmosphere.

TWIN PLANETS?
Venus and Earth are sometimes called twins because they are a similar size. But in many ways, they are very different. Fill in the fact cards to reveal just how alike or different the two planets are.

Mostly carbon dioxide

Plants and animals

60°F (15°C)

Mostly nitrogen and oxygen

900°F (475°C)

No life

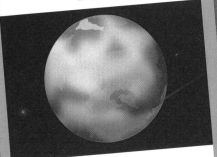

EARTH

AVERAGE DIAMETER: 7,926 miles (12,756 km)

ATMOSPHERE: ....
....

SURFACE TEMPERATURE: ....

LIFE: ....
....

VENUS

AVERAGE DIAMETER: 7,521 miles (12,104 km)

ATMOSPHERE: ....
....

SURFACE TEMPERATURE: ....

LIFE: ....
....

VENUS

Average diameter:
7,521 miles (12,104 km)

Average distance from Sun: 0.7 AU

Year: 225 Earth days

Day: 243 Earth days

Moons: 0

WHERE IS VENUS?

Use what you've learned about the size and temperature of Venus to work out which numbered planet it is on this graph. Read the left-hand page again if you get stuck!

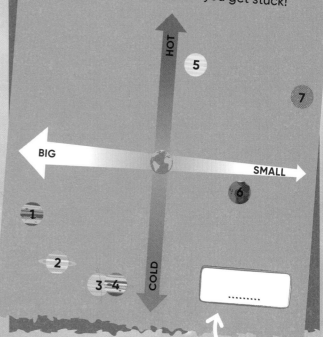

WRITE IT!

The atmosphere
A thick atmosphere covers the whole planet, so the surface can't be seen without special imaging equipment or radar. Pressure on the surface is about 100 times that on Earth.

WHY SO HOT?

The atmosphere of Venus is 96 percent carbon dioxide—a greenhouse gas that traps heat and stops it from escaping the planet. Use the key below to complete this diagram that shows why Venus is scorchingly hot.

Coloring key

1 Sunlight

2 Heat

3 Sulfuric acid clouds

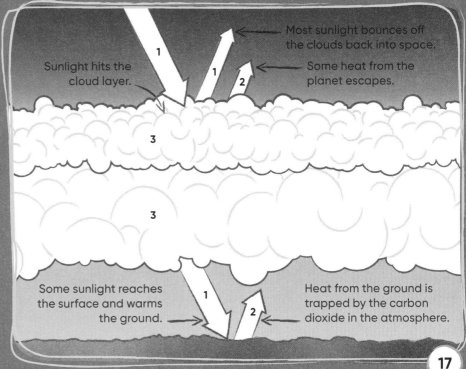

Most sunlight bounces off the clouds back into space.

Sunlight hits the cloud layer.

Some heat from the planet escapes.

Some sunlight reaches the surface and warms the ground.

Heat from the ground is trapped by the carbon dioxide in the atmosphere.

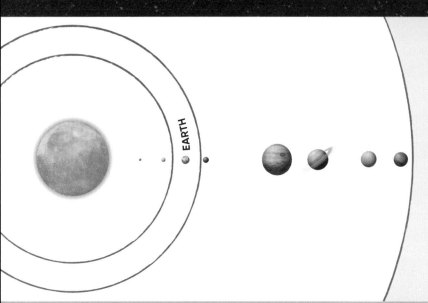

WHERE IS IT JUST RIGHT?

Earth sits in an area scientists sometimes call the "Goldilocks zone," because it's neither too hot nor too cold—it's just right. This moderate temperature is one of the things that enables life on Earth to survive. Use the key to color in this diagram of the temperature zones in our Solar System.

Coloring key

〰 Too hot

〰 Just right

〰 Too cold

COLOR IT!

EARTH

Our planet is just one among many, but it is also unique—no other planet is known to support life. So far, Earth is the only planet shown to have liquid water permanently present on its surface. This, along with a moderate surface temperature, is what allows life to thrive here.

Planet Earth

Earth is made of a mixture of metal and rock. Inside, it is split into layers, like an onion. Water is present on its surface in all three forms: liquid, solid (snow and ice), and gas (as water vapor).

EARTH FORMED AROUND 4.5 BILLION YEARS AGO.

Water in vapor form (gas) makes clouds in the skies around our planet.

Liquid water forms oceans, lakes, and rivers on Earth's surface.

EARTH

Average diameter:
7,926 miles (12,756 km)

Average distance from Sun: 1 AU

Year: 365.242 days

Day: 24 hours

Moons: 1

EXOSPHERE, 400–6,000 MILES (600–10,000 KM)

DRAW IT!

THERMOSPHERE, 50–400 MILES (80–600 KM)

MESOSPHERE, 30–50 MILES (50–80 KM)

TROPOSPHERE, 0–10 MILES (0–16 KM)

STRATOSPHERE, 10–30 MILES (16–50 KM)

WHAT HAPPENS WHERE?

Earth's atmosphere is split into five layers, going up and out from the planet's surface. Different items can be found in each of these layers. Read the information below, then draw each thing in its correct layer (not shown to scale) on the left.

SPACE STATION

The International Space Station orbits Earth at about 250 miles (400 km) up, in the hottest layer, where temperatures reach 4,500°F (2,500°C).

METEORS

Meteors or "shooting stars" can be seen in the third layer up, as space rocks burn up. It is the coldest layer, with temperatures as low as -280°F (-170°C).

WEATHER

Earth's weather circulates in this layer—clouds form and rain falls. It is the layer closest to our planet and contains the air we breathe.

SATELLITES

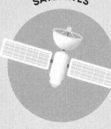

Many satellites orbit in the outside layer, which extends about 2.6 percent of the way to the Moon. It is where Earth's atmosphere blends into open space.

PLANES

Commercial jets fly where there's less turbulence—above the weather. This same layer also contains the ozone that protects us from the Sun's ultraviolet rays.

19

MATCH THE LUNAR CRATERS

The Moon is covered in thousands of craters. These diagrams show how craters form. Draw lines to match each description of a crater to the correct image.

1 Space rock
A meteoroid hurtles toward the Moon's surface.

2 Impact
The initial impact creates shock waves and vaporizes the meteoroid.

3 Explosion
The shock waves force out material from the landing site, spreading it over the nearby landscape.

4 Crater
A crater is formed. Large craters may contain a central peak.

MATCH IT!

OUR MOON

Earth's moon is a small, rocky body that orbits our planet. It formed around 4.5 billion years ago, when a space object hit the Earth and the resulting rocky debris became the Moon. The Moon is the only other object in our Solar System that humans have walked on.

Bowl-shaped dents, called craters, are where meteoroids and comets have hit the Moon.

Lighter areas are known as lunar highlands.

Dark areas called mares (seas) show where lava once covered the Moon's surface.

Earth's moon
The Moon is the only space object whose features can be seen from Earth without any special equipment. It has no atmosphere, which means even the tiniest meteoroids are able to crash into its surface.

PEOPLE HAVE NOT WALKED ON THE **MOON'S SURFACE** SINCE **1972.**

Moon on the move

The Moon spins counterclockwise on its axis while moving in orbit around Earth. It takes 27.3 days for the Moon to make one orbit, and the same time for it to spin once, which means that we always see the same side of the Moon from Earth.

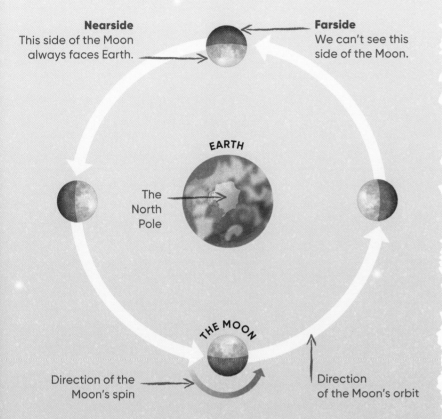

Nearside
This side of the Moon always faces Earth.

Farside
We can't see this side of the Moon.

EARTH

The North Pole

THE MOON

Direction of the Moon's spin

Direction of the Moon's orbit

WHICH SIDE?

Unscramble the letters inside each of these pictures to spell out which view of the Moon is shown in each of them.

WRITE IT!

a _ _ _ _ _ _ _ _

b _ _ _ _ _ _ _

COLOR IT!

COMPLETE THE PHASES

As the Moon orbits Earth, we see different portions of its sunlit half—so it looks like the Moon changes shape. These eight circles show the eight shapes, or "phases," of the Moon that we see from Earth. Use the key to help you color them in correctly.

Coloring key

Unlit area

Sunlit portion visible from Earth

New Moon
The brightly lit half of the Moon is turned away from Earth, so we can't see it.

Waxing crescent
As the Moon moves counterclockwise, we can see a sliver of its sunlit half.

First quarter
About half of the Moon is visible. It has completed a quarter of its orbit of Earth.

Waxing gibbous
More than half the Moon can be seen from Earth.

Full Moon
The half that is brightly lit by the Sun is now facing fully toward Earth.

Waning gibbous
The visible part of the Moon begins to shrink, or "wane."

Last quarter
The Moon has traveled three-quarters of its orbit, and half of it is visible to us.

Waning crescent
A thin sliver of the Moon can be seen, and the Moon has nearly completed its orbit.

21

ECLIPSES

An eclipse occurs when the Sun, Earth, and Moon line up, casting shadows on each other. Sometimes the Moon can completely block our view of the Sun, while Earth's shadow can make the Moon glow red.

How an eclipse works
There are two main types of eclipse: lunar and solar. These diagrams show what happens during each of them.

Total solar eclipse
In a small area of Earth, the Sun's light is completely blocked.

SUN

MOON

EARTH

Solar eclipse
A solar eclipse occurs when the Moon passes between Earth and the Sun, blocking the Sun's light and casting a shadow on Earth.

Partial solar eclipse
Over a larger area of Earth's surface, some of the Sun is still visible.

COLOR IT!

FINISH THE ECLIPSE
During a solar eclipse, we see the Moon move steadily across the Sun's disk. These images show what happens as the Moon moves across the Sun. Complete the sequence, using black to draw the mirror images of each stage onto the empty disks.

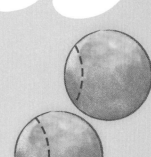

BONUS QUESTION
Can you name the type of solar eclipse where there's a ring of orange light?

....

NAME THAT SHADOW

Complete the row of lunar eclipse shadows running across the Earth and ignore those letters. Unjumble the remaining letters and write down the name of a type of shadow.

_ _ _ _ _ _ _ _

P E S E
P R
M I N
L A B
C U
E

NEVER LOOK DIRECTLY AT THE SUN, EVEN DURING AN ECLIPSE. DOING THIS CAN DAMAGE YOUR EYES.

Lunar eclipse
When Earth is between the Sun and Moon, it can cast a shadow on the Moon, creating a lunar eclipse. The Moon appears to glow red, because Earth's atmosphere scatters other colors of light away so that only red light is left.

SUN

If the Moon is in the umbra, there is a **total lunar eclipse**.

Umbra (full shadow)

EARTH

MOON

Penumbra (partial shadow)

If the Moon is in the penumbra, there is a **partial lunar eclipse**.

WHICH EFFECT IS WHICH?

A number of amazing sights can occur during different stages of a total solar eclipse. Some of them are described below. Can you match each description to the right image?

MATCH IT!

a

b

c

d

e

Sun's corona
When the Moon entirely covers the Sun, the corona (part of the Sun's atmosphere) flares out at the edges.

Partial solar eclipse
This happens when the Moon moves in front of the Sun, blocking only part of the Sun as seen from the Earth.

Diamond ring effect
When one spot of sunlight appears with a thin ring of light around the edge of the Moon, it looks like a diamond ring.

Annular solar eclipse
If the Moon's disk is too small to entirely cover the Sun, it creates a thick ring of glowing orange-red light.

Baily's beads
Tiny patches of sunlight can appear around the edges of the Moon, just before and after it covers the Sun.

MARS

Mars is the planet most similar to Earth, but it is far from the same—its surface is coated in red-colored dust and can be freezing cold. While it seems that water once flowed on Mars, all the water present there today is in the form of ice or vapor.

The planet Mars

Mars's surface looks remarkably similar to Earth's, with open deserts, towering cliffs, dry riverbeds, extinct volcanoes, and other features that look very familiar to us. Of all the planets in the Solar System, this one is most like our own.

Mars has a cap of frozen carbon dioxide at both poles.

Olympus Mons is a volcano—the largest in our Solar System.

DAYS ON MARS ARE NEARLY THE SAME LENGTH AS THOSE ON EARTH.

The Valles Marineris is a huge crack 2,490 miles (4,000 km) long.

COLOR THE PLANET

This scene looks a little like one you'd find on Earth. But try coloring it in using the key below to see just how different a day on Mars looks and find out why it's called the red planet.

Coloring Key
1 Surface
2 Valley
3 Sky
4 Rover

COLOR IT!

GREETINGS FROM MARS

MARS

Average diameter: 4,217 miles (6,786 km)
Average distance from Sun: 1.5 AU
Year: 687 Earth days
Day: 24.5 Earth hours
Moons: 2

Mars's surface is dusty and appears brownish red due to iron oxide in the rocks.

Carbon dioxide is the main gas in the planet's thin atmosphere. Mars's winds can cause dust storms on the surface.

NAME IT!

16-8-15-2-15-19

a _ _ _ _ _ _

4-5-9-13-15-19

b _ _ _ _ _ _

NAME THE MOONS

Mars's moons are small and shaped a bit like potatoes. They may once have been asteroids that became trapped by the planet's gravity. To find the names of the two moons, replace each number with a letter. A = 1, B = 2, C = 3, and so on.

FIND IT!

LOCATE THE LIQUID WATER

Scientists have been looking for liquid water on Mars using radar. They finally found it at the poles, but can you spot it? Draw frozen circles around the ice to find the single patch of liquid water that isn't frozen or covered by a boulder.

Key

❄ Ice
🔴 Boulder

ASTEROIDS

Our Solar System is home to a large number of rocky and metallic objects, which travel in orbit around the Sun. These lumps of space rock are called asteroids. They are covered in craters from where they have smashed into each other.

Where are they?

Most of the asteroids in our Solar System orbit the Sun in an area between the orbits of Mars and Jupiter called the Main Asteroid Belt. A special type called trojans share their orbit with a planet, like Jupiter, Mars, Neptune, and Earth.

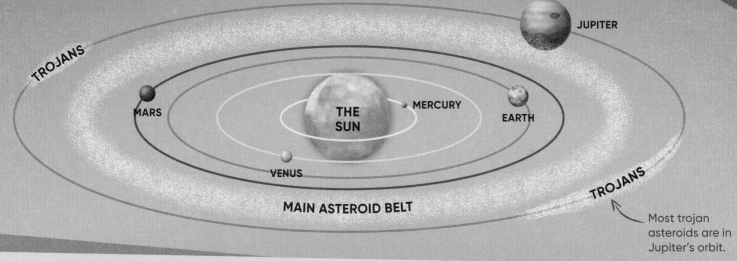

TROJANS

JUPITER

MARS

THE SUN

MERCURY

EARTH

VENUS

MAIN ASTEROID BELT

TROJANS

Most trojan asteroids are in Jupiter's orbit.

FIND THE ASTEROIDS

Work out where some asteroids are hidden in this diagram. They must be next to a plus sign (+) but can't be next to a minus sign (–). Here's an example:

1. Start by crossing out all the squares touching a (–) box.

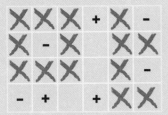

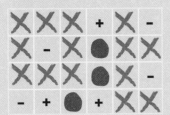

2. Draw asteroids in all the empty squares that are next to a (+) box.

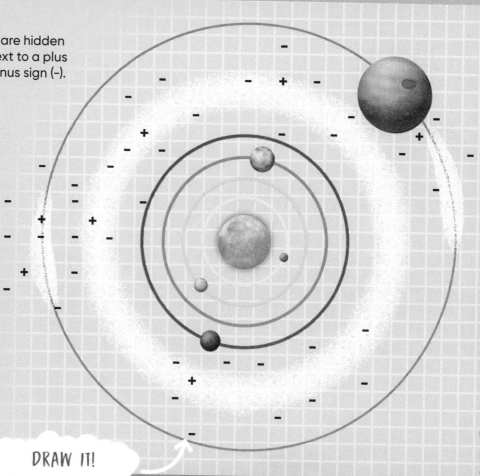

DRAW IT!

WHICH IS WHICH?

Asteroids come in a range of shapes and sizes. Can you match the descriptions of notable asteroids below to the correct image?

MATCH IT!

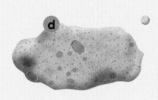

Toutatis
This asteroid is 3 miles (5 km) long and is an irregular shape. It takes four years to orbit the Sun.

Ceres
The largest asteroid in the Solar System, this spherical (round) asteroid is also classed as a dwarf planet.

Kleopatra
This bone-shaped metallic asteroid contains a mixture of iron and nickel.

Ida
This asteroid has its own moon—another asteroid, which is called Dactyl.

COLOR THE ORBITS

Most asteroids stay in the Asteroid Belt, but some have wide, more oval-shaped orbits, bringing them closer to Earth. Choose a different color for each asteroid in the key below, then use the colors to fill in each of the asteroids and their orbits.

THE FIRST **ASTEROID** EVER DISCOVERED WAS **CERES** —IN 1801.

Key

Toutatis

Ida

Itokawa

Ceres

Eros

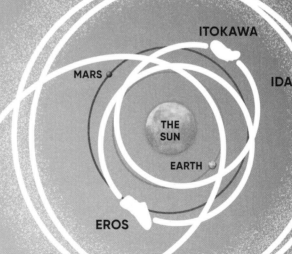

ITOKAWA

IDA

MARS

THE SUN

CERES

EARTH

EROS

TOUTATIS

COLOR IT!

JUPITER

Average diameter: 88,846 miles (142,984 km)

Average distance from Sun: 5.2 AU

Year: 11.9 Earth years

Day: 10 Earth hours

Moons: 80

JUPITER

The fifth planet from the Sun is a gas giant and the largest planet in the Solar System. In fact, Jupiter is two times bigger than all the other planets put together! Its outer layer has striped clouds dotted with storms.

The planet Jupiter
Jupiter's clouds are icy, but the center of the planet is hotter than the Sun. The planet has a dust ring around it, but this ring is so faint that it wasn't detected until a spacecraft visited Jupiter in 1979.

The Great Red Spot is a massive storm that has been raging for at least 200 years.

Jupiter's clouds contain ammonia, water, methane, and hydrogen sulfide.

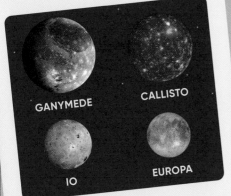

GANYMEDE

CALLISTO

IO

EUROPA

Jupiter's moons
There are 80 known moons in orbit around Jupiter. Ganymede is the largest moon in our Solar System and is larger than the planet Mercury. Io is the most volcanic place in the Solar System, while Callisto is covered in the most craters. Europa may have liquid water under its icy crust.

Storms often appear in the cloud layer above Jupiter's surface.

DRAW IT!

JUPITER

JUST HOW BIG IS JUPITER?

What numbers do the symbols below stand for? Check these pages for the answer! Then solve the equation to find out how many planet Earths fit across Jupiter's diameter and draw them in.

Object key

▲ The number of moons around Jupiter

● Jupiter's number in the order of planets from the Sun

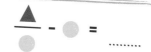

$$\frac{\blacktriangle}{\bullet} - \bullet = \ldots\ldots$$

JUPITER IS
318
TIMES
MORE
MASSIVE
THAN EARTH.

FIND IT!

FIND THE WORDS

Can you find the Jupiter-related words hidden in the word search? Use the words inside the box below to help you.

Gas giant   Cloud bands

Io

Great Red Spot   Ganymede

Europa   Callisto

```
        J A P Z
      B W P G K G T Y
    S I R O A P A G W Q
  E A F B H T S I N P N B D
  E U F A H S G I Y N O I M B
X J R G U I I V M Y M R I S
L S X O G L A S E M Y A U J
D E R X P L N G D E C G F E
U L G R E A T R E D S P O T
W D V S C S R N E D M O
  O B C L O U D B A N D S
  X Z C Y T V M O P R
    N A I G S A G V
        Y H K E
```

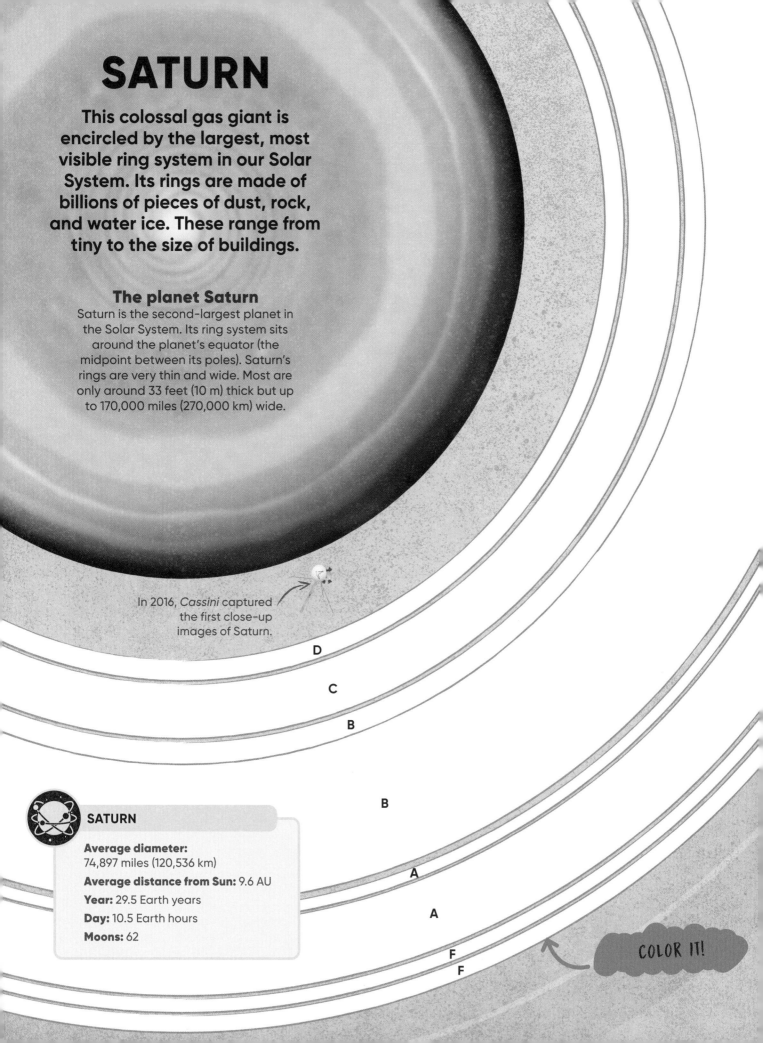

SATURN

This colossal gas giant is encircled by the largest, most visible ring system in our Solar System. Its rings are made of billions of pieces of dust, rock, and water ice. These range from tiny to the size of buildings.

The planet Saturn

Saturn is the second-largest planet in the Solar System. Its ring system sits around the planet's equator (the midpoint between its poles). Saturn's rings are very thin and wide. Most are only around 33 feet (10 m) thick but up to 170,000 miles (270,000 km) wide.

In 2016, *Cassini* captured the first close-up images of Saturn.

D

C

B

B

SATURN

Average diameter:
74,897 miles (120,536 km)

Average distance from Sun: 9.6 AU

Year: 29.5 Earth years

Day: 10.5 Earth hours

Moons: 62

A

A

F

F

COLOR IT!

COMPLETE THE RINGS

Saturn's rings are named after the letters of the alphabet, in the order they were discovered. The gaps between them are named after famous astronomers. Use the key to help you complete this image of the inner ring system.

Color by letter

〰 A ring

〰 B ring

C ring

〰 D ring

〰 F ring

The biggest gap, called the Cassini Division, is between the A and B rings.

Saturn's rings have lots of gaps between them. Some also have moons, which keep the gaps clear.

REVEAL THE MOON

Like Jupiter, Saturn is surrounded by lots of small moons. It also has a number of inner moons, which orbit the planet within the ring system. One moon is much larger than all of the others. Cross out the letters of the word "SATURN" in order to reveal the name of this moon.

S T I A T T U A R N N

_ _ _ _ _

WRITE IT!

DESIGN A RING SYSTEM

Design your own ring system around this planet. Try varying the size of the rings so that they are not all the same width. If you'd like, you could add a few moons as well.

Rings of ice and rock
The material in the rings may be from broken asteroids, comets, and moons.

DRAW IT!

URANUS

This ice giant is the coldest planet in the Solar System, with temperatures that can plummet to -371°F (-224°C). It is the third largest planet in the Solar System and the second farthest from the Sun.

URANUS

Average diameter: 31,763 miles (51,118 km)
Average distance from Sun: 19.2 AU
Year: 84 Earth years
Day: 17 Earth hours
Moons: 27

The planet Uranus

Although Uranus's atmosphere is a mix of gases, the planet is made mainly of heavier "icy" materials—water, methane, and ammonia. It has few features, other than some white clouds. These may be methane ice, a solid form of methane gas only found when it's very cold.

Clouds move around the surface, carried by winds and the planet's rotation.

Methane gas in Uranus's atmosphere makes the planet appear blue.

TILT THE PLANET

Most planets spin on a vertical (upright) axis, but Uranus rotates on a horizontal (sideways) axis. Scientists think it was knocked on its side by a rock the size of Earth. Look at how the three other planets rotate, then draw in the arrows to show Uranus's axis.

MERCURY

EARTH

DRAW IT!

JUPITER

URANUS

URANUS WAS THE FIRST **PLANET** DISCOVERED WITH THE USE OF A **TELESCOPE.**

COMPLETE THE CRYSTAL

Uranus is incredibly cold! Build this ice crystal to show the two substances that, along with water, make up most of this frosty planet's mass.

EN
D
RO
UM
HE
G
HY
LI

COMPLETE IT!

This spot on the planet is likely to be a huge storm.

NAME IT!

EARTH
WOULD BE ABLE
TO FIT INSIDE
URANUS
63 TIMES.

Uranus's 13 rings are thin and hard to see; they were only discovered in 1977.

WHICH MOON IS WHICH?

Uranus has 27 moons, many named after characters from the plays of William Shakespeare. Here, they have been laid out from biggest to smallest. The names of the six largest moons have been removed. Use the information in the box below to work out which is which.

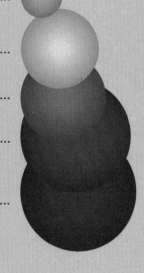

TRINCULO
CUPID
FERDINAND
MARGARET
FRANCISCO
MAB
PERDITA
STEPHANO
CORDELIA
OPHELIA
SETEBOS
PROSPERO
BIANCA
DESDEMONA
CALIBAN
ROSALIND
CRESSIDA
BELINDA
JULIET
PORTIA
SYCORAX

a ....
b ....
c ....
d ....
e ....
f ....

ARIEL: 720 MI (1,158 KM) WIDE

UMBRIEL: 726 MI (1,169 KM) WIDE

MIRANDA: 293 MI (472 KM) WIDE

OBERON: 946 MI (1,523 KM) WIDE

TITANIA: 981 MI (1,578 KM) WIDE

PUCK: 101 MI (162 KM) WIDE

NEPTUNE

This ice giant is the farthest planet from the Sun—in fact, it is so far away that it wasn't discovered until 1846. Neptune is the smallest of the four giant planets, but it is still around four times bigger than planet Earth.

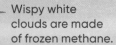

TRITON ACCOUNTS FOR **99.7%** OF THE TOTAL MASS OF NEPTUNE'S 14 MOONS.

The planet Neptune

This cold, blue planet is mostly a mix of water, liquid ammonia, and liquid methane. Its atmosphere has clouds, strong winds, and turbulent storms. Neptune's one large moon, Triton, is significantly wider than all of the planet's 13 other known moons.

Wispy white clouds are made of frozen methane.

Dark spots show storms in the atmosphere; winds can reach over 700 mph (1,200 kph).

At least five faint dust rings surround the planet.

The blue color is caused by methane gas in the atmosphere.

NEPTUNE

Average diameter:
30,775 miles (49,528 km)

Average distance from Sun: 30 AU

Year: 165 Earth years

Day: 16 Earth hours

Moons: 14

COMPLETE THE TIMELINE

In 1977, NASA launched two *Voyager* spacecrafts to explore the outer planets of the Solar System. They became the first two spacecrafts to travel beyond the planets. The first images we have of Neptune (and Uranus) were taken by *Voyager 2*. Use the words in the box below to label this timeline of the *Voyager 2* mission.

LABEL IT!

Neptune   Jupiter   Saturn   Uranus

BLAST-OFF!

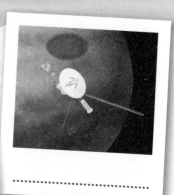

....

1977

Voyager 2 is launched. This is before *Voyager 1*, but it is due to reach the outer planets second.

1979

Both crafts take photos of a huge gas giant, its Great Red Spot, and eruptions on its moon Io.

VOYAGER'S VOYAGE?

The spacecraft *Voyager 2* has traveled beyond the planets. To get there, it went past Jupiter, Saturn, Uranus, and Neptune, taking detailed pictures of each planet to send back to Earth. Which one of these tangled routes takes you past these planets and out beyond?

FOLLOW IT!

JUPITER

SATURN

URANUS

NEPTUNE

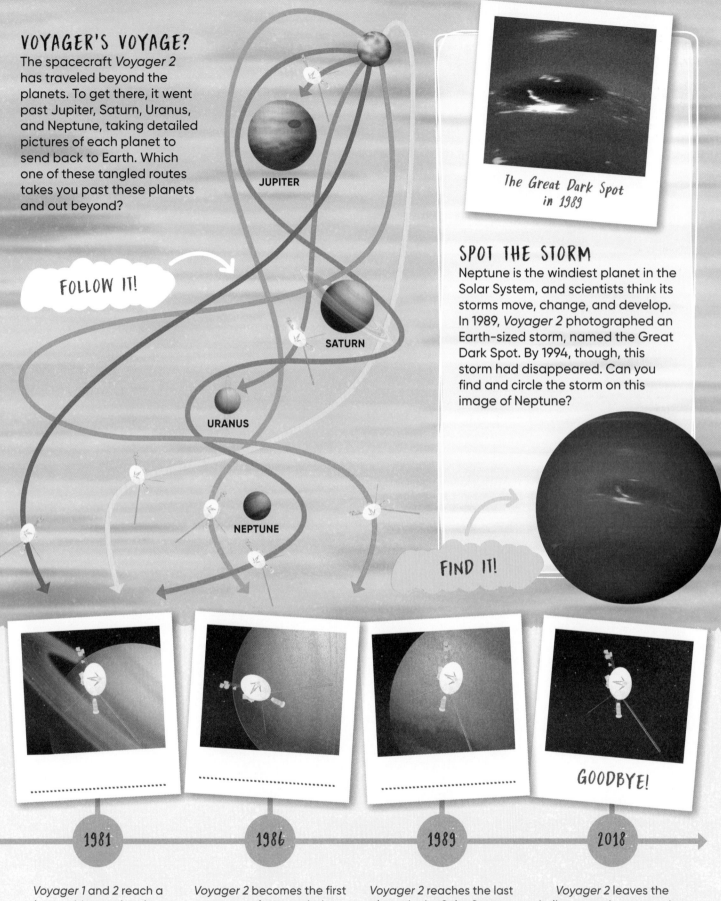

The Great Dark Spot in 1989

SPOT THE STORM

Neptune is the windiest planet in the Solar System, and scientists think its storms move, change, and develop. In 1989, *Voyager 2* photographed an Earth-sized storm, named the Great Dark Spot. By 1994, though, this storm had disappeared. Can you find and circle the storm on this image of Neptune?

FIND IT!

GOODBYE!

1981

Voyager 1 and 2 reach a planet with stunning rings. They photograph the planet and some of its moons.

1986

Voyager 2 becomes the first spacecraft to reach the seventh planet in our Solar System, an icy giant.

1989

Voyager 2 reaches the last planet in the Solar System. It takes photos of the Great Dark Spot storm.

2018

Voyager 2 leaves the heliopause, the outer edge of the Sun's atmosphere, around 120 AU from the Sun.

DWARF PLANETS

Our Solar System contains five known dwarf planets. Just like planets, they orbit the Sun and are big enough that their gravity has made them spherical. Unlike planets, however, whose gravity is strong enough to clear their orbits of nearby objects (usually by deflecting them out of the way), dwarf planets have too little gravity to achieve this.

DRAW IT!

HOW BIG IS PLUTO?

Can you show just how small Pluto is? Use the diameter given in Pluto's fact panel below to draw its outline compared to this map of Australia. The center is marked for you, and you can find the planet's radius by halving its diameter.

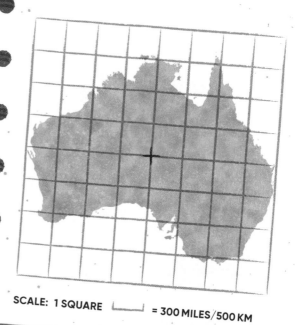

SCALE: 1 SQUARE ⌞___⌟ = 300 MILES/500 KM

Pluto

Pluto orbits the Sun in the Kuiper Belt—a ring of icy objects beyond the orbit of Neptune. Pluto used to be known as the ninth planet in our Solar System. However, in 2006, it was reclassified to dwarf planet status, because it does not have enough gravity to clear other objects from its orbit.

BONUS QUESTION

Beyond the orbit of Neptune is a ring of icy rocks. Four of the five known dwarf planets can be found here. But what is it called?

....

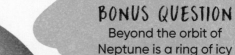

PLUTO

Average diameter: 1,473 miles (2,370 km)

Average distance from Sun: 39 AU

Year: 248 Earth years

Day: 153 Earth hours

Moons: 5

The surface of this frozen dwarf planet is covered in ice.

PLUTO MAY HAVE CRYOVOLCANOES— **VOLCANOES THAT ERUPT** A MIXTURE OF **ICE AND GAS.**

WHAT IS IT?

Use what you've learned about different space objects and the words in the box below to help you complete this flow chart.

Moon

Asteroid

Dwarf planet

Planet

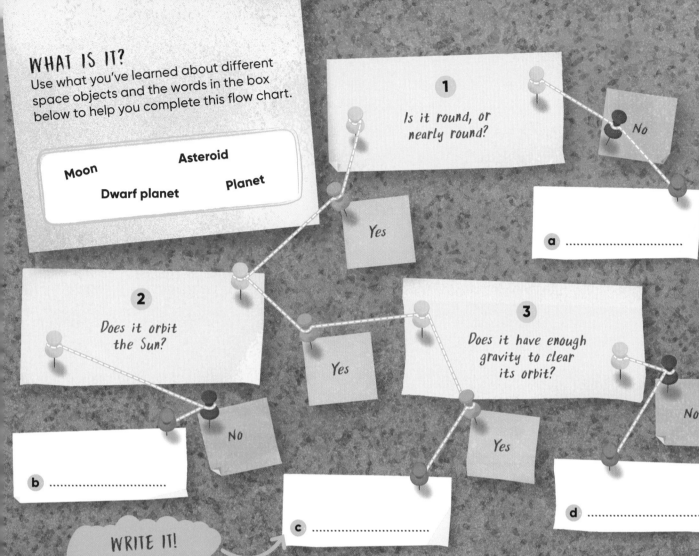

1 Is it round, or nearly round?

No

Yes

a ....

2 Does it orbit the Sun?

No

Yes

b ....

3 Does it have enough gravity to clear its orbit?

Yes

No

c ....

d ....

WRITE IT!

SORT THE DWARF PLANETS

Can you match these descriptions to the correct dwarf planets?

MATCH IT!

Pluto
Once considered the ninth planet, this icy world is the best known of the dwarf planets.

Ceres
This heavily cratered object makes up nearly one-third of all the material in the main asteroid belt.

Haumea
This dwarf planet rotates so fast, it has flattened to become egg-shaped. It has two moons.

Eris
Around the same size as Pluto, this object has one small moon and takes 557 Earth days to orbit the Sun.

Makemake
Found among the icy objects of the Kuiper Belt, this dwarf planet's surface is reddish brown.

COMETS

From Earth, comets appear as bright streaks of light across the sky. In fact, they are dense balls of ice, rock, and dust that grow glowing tails only when they are close to the Sun. Comets move constantly in wide, looping orbits around the Sun.

Comet structure

The heart of a comet is called the nucleus. As a comet approaches the Sun, the frozen gas, dust, and ice that make up the nucleus heat up and form a cloud around it called the coma. Closer to the Sun, radiation and solar wind blast toward the comet, creating two tails—one of gas and one of dust.

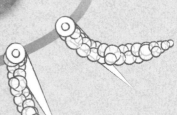

Nucleus
The center of the comet is a hard ball of dust, rock, ice, and frozen gases.

Coma
This layer around the nucleus forms when gas and dust are released from the nucleus.

Gas tail
Gases released from the comet's nucleus form a straight tail, which points away from the Sun.

COLOR IT!

COLOR THE TAILS

As a comet orbits the Sun, its two tails grow and move. Use the key to help you complete this diagram of a comet's orbit around the Sun.

Coloring key
Dust tail
Gas tail
Nucleus
Coma

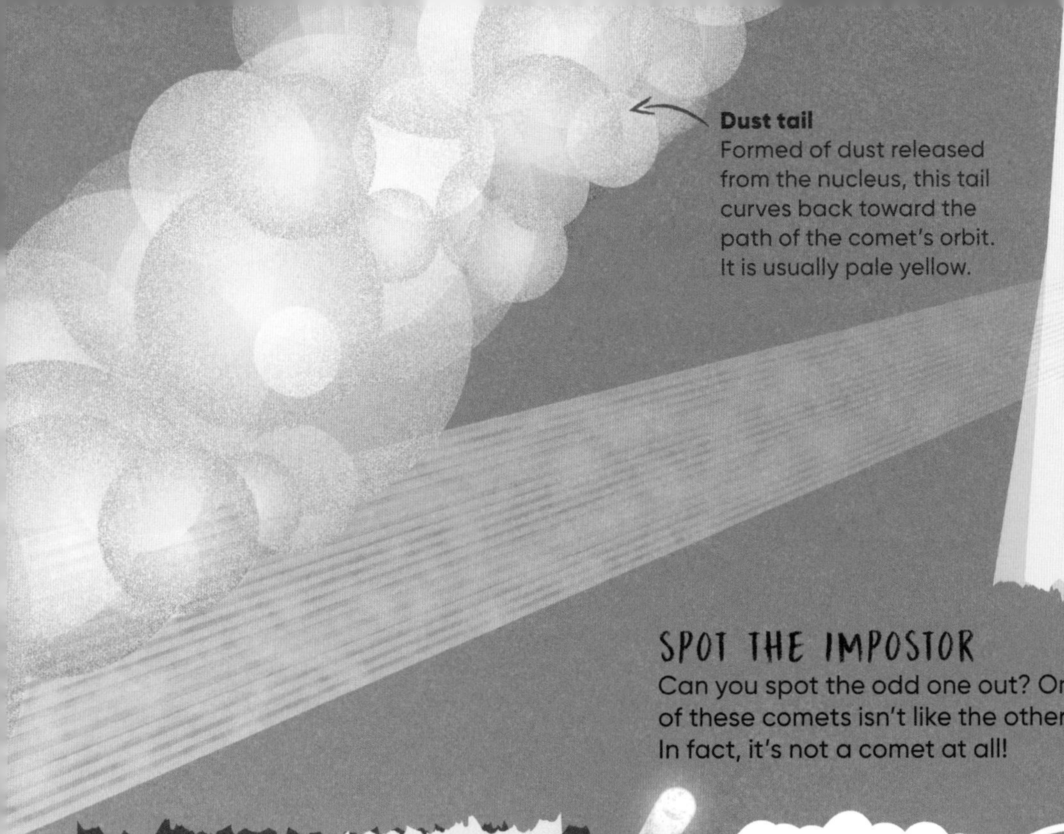

Dust tail
Formed of dust released from the nucleus, this tail curves back toward the path of the comet's orbit. It is usually pale yellow.

Hale-Bopp Comet
The twin tails of this unusually bright comet were visible when it passed close by Earth in 1997.

SPOT THE IMPOSTOR
Can you spot the odd one out? One of these comets isn't like the others. In fact, it's not a comet at all!

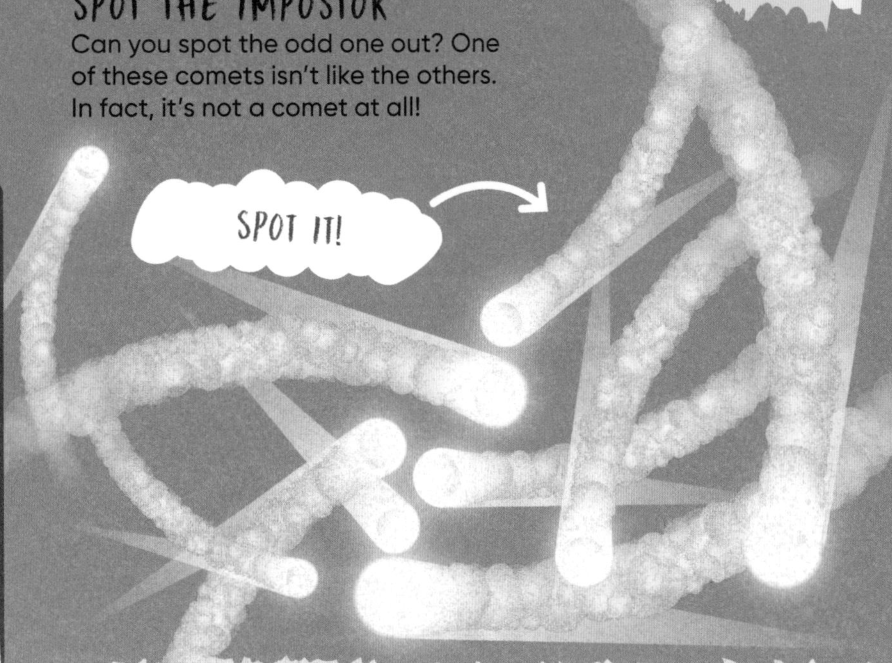

SPOT IT!

WHAT YEARS?
The most famous comet is Halley's Comet, named after the astronomer Edmond Halley in 1682. He was the first person to work out that some comets reappear at regular intervals as they travel past Earth. Halley's Comet was seen in 1531, then returned every 75 or 76 years. Can you circle the three years below in which the comet returned?

(1531) 1533 1540
1541 1545 1580
1589 1607
1627
1660 1663
1682 1699
1735 1741
1758 1770

FIND THE NAME
What is the name of the cloud of gases around a comet's nucleus? Cross out the letters in the words COMET and TAIL below, then rearrange the remaining letters to spell the answer.

_ _ _ _

FIND IT!

C T O M O A I

C A E T L M

METEORITES

Space rocks that manage to travel through Earth's atmosphere and reach the ground are called meteorites. They come in all shapes and sizes—some are tiny pebbles, while others are colossal rocks the size of cars. Meteorites can be stony or made of metals, such as nickel and iron.

Name-changing rocks

Space rocks are named depending on their size and where they are in relation to Earth. A large, irregular rocky or metallic object in space (that is not a moon) is an asteroid. Asteroids that are less than 3 feet (1 m) across are meteoroids. The streak of light from a meteoroid burning up in Earth's atmosphere is a meteor, and a rock that hits Earth's surface is a meteorite.

MATCH THE METEORITES

Meteorites can be divided into three categories, depending on what they are made of. Can you match the descriptions of meteorites below to the correct image?

Iron
These meteorites are the cores of ancient asteroids. Many have criss-cross patterns of metal crystals.

Stony-iron
The multicolored patches on this meteorite are from different areas of metal and stone.

Stony
These meteorites are solid rock. They are darker on the outside than inside due to their fiery journey through the atmosphere.

REARRANGE IT!

When a large meteorite hits the ground, it can create a bowl-shaped dent. Rearrange the letters here to spell the proper name for this dent.

A R
R E C
R T

_ _ _ _ _ _

WRITE IT!

MATCH IT!

METEOROID

METEOR

SPACE

ATMOSPHERE

METEORITE

EARTH

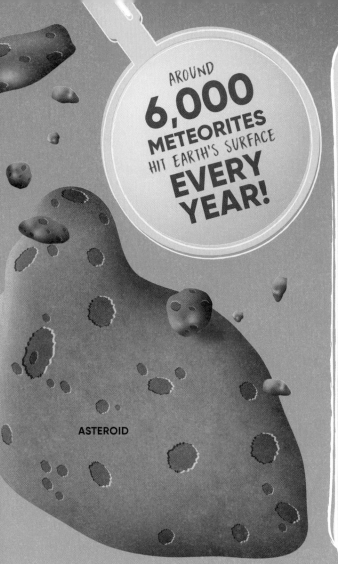

AROUND 6,000 METEORITES HIT EARTH'S SURFACE EVERY YEAR!

ASTEROID

NAME THAT ROCK

Look at the size and position of these space rocks. Then use the word box and what you've learned so far to help you fill in the labels.

Meteor

Asteroid

Meteoroid

Meteorite

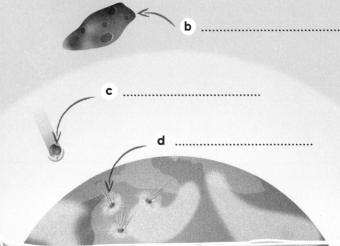

NAME IT!

a ....

b ....

c ....

d ....

DRAW A METEOR SHOWER

A meteor shower occurs when lots of meteors fall together through Earth's atmosphere. Use this image of the Perseid meteor shower, which happens every year between mid-July and the end of August, to help you draw your own meteor shower in the sky.

1. Your meteors should be pointing toward Earth, with their tails streaking up toward space. They don't all need to point in exactly the same direction.

2. Remember, stars will still be visible behind your meteors.

3. Once your stars and meteors are in place, fill in the night sky around them.

DRAW IT!

The Perseid meteor shower

STARS

From Earth, stars appear as twinkly, shining lights in the night sky. Up close, there's nothing twinkly about them. Each star is a ball of very hot gas, with huge amounts of energy in its core. This energy travels out of the star and into space in the form of light, heat, and other types of radiation.

Star types

Stars vary in size, brightness, color, and lifespan. This graph shows the temperature of different types of stars and the amount of light they emit. Most stars occupy an area in the center of the chart called the "main sequence."

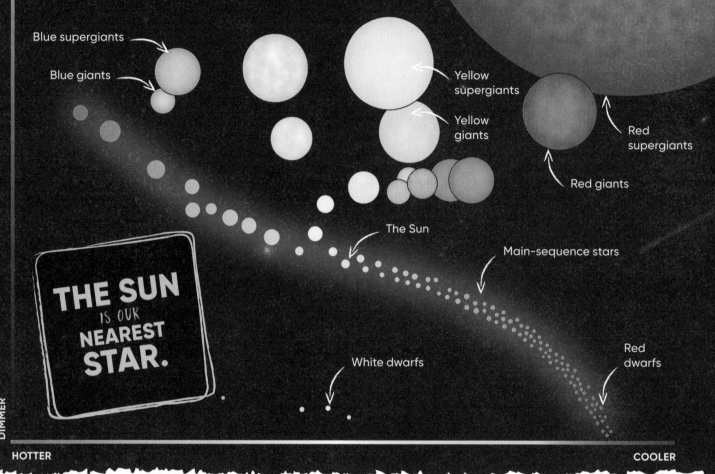

Blue supergiants

Blue giants

Yellow supergiants

Yellow giants

Red supergiants

Red giants

The Sun

Main-sequence stars

Red dwarfs

White dwarfs

THE SUN IS OUR NEAREST STAR.

DIMMER

HOTTER   COOLER

HOW HOT ARE THEY?

A star's color is determined by how hot its surface is. Use the key to complete this chart showing which color occurs at which temperature.

Color by number
1   2   3   4
5   6   7

COLOR IT!

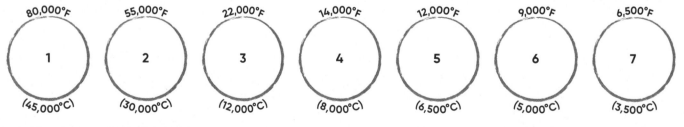

80,000°F	55,000°F	22,000°F	14,000°F	12,000°F	9,000°F	6,500°F
1	2	3	4	5	6	7
(45,000°C)	(30,000°C)	(12,000°C)	(8,000°C)	(6,500°C)	(5,000°C)	(3,500°C)

← HOTTER STARS   COOLER STARS →

FIND THE STARS

Find the names of the different star types, which have been hidden in the word search to the right.

```
G A B S F J Q O S Y J W I Z V B
Y V K R E D S U P E R G I A N T
S B Q M B F U X K L W I P B N A
F D X C L S V B K L S J A H Y W
U R Y R U V M Q E O V W N A F L
K L T W E R E T N W P I O R V U
A B N G S D B G G S G G A X H G
F Y A G U S D L G U G W N S Y G
G J I R P D A W U P D W R B R T
K Q G D E E F W A E Q F A W I U
W V W V R D U Y T R G P H D O T
C U O S G J G I X G F I I W S G
G O L C I H H I U I E W A O N A
Z B L Y A W G L A A D F Q N F B
W M E E N B E K O N F J G R T I
U T Y Q T A S G C T T W I M P B
```

Blue supergiant

Yellow giant

Red giant

Red dwarf

Red supergiant

Blue giant   White dwarf

Yellow supergiant

FIND IT!

PROXIMA CENTAURI

TYPE: *Red dwarf*

COLOR: ....

SIZE: *0.14 times the Sun's diameter*

DISTANCE FROM EARTH: ....

BETELGEUSE

TYPE: ....

COLOR: *Red*

SIZE: *764 times the Sun's diameter*

DISTANCE FROM EARTH: *600 light-years*

SIRIUS A

TYPE: ....

COLOR: *White*

SIZE: ....

DISTANCE FROM EARTH: *8.6 light-years*

WRITE IT!

FILL IN THE MISSING FACTS

Our nearest star is the Sun. Here are fact files about a few other major stars. Use the box on the right to help you complete the missing information.

1.7 times the Sun's diameter

Orange-red

4.4 light-years

Red supergiant

White main-sequence star

LIFE CYCLE OF A STAR

Stars don't stay the same for their whole existence. Stars begin inside a huge cloud of gas and dust called a nebula. But after that, their life cycle depends on their mass (how much matter they contain). Very massive stars shine brightly, but for a shorter time than less massive stars. The end of a star's life also varies.

Life stages

Gravity causes spinning balls of gas called protostars to form inside a nebula. Pressure makes these denser and hotter until nuclear reactions begin inside them, creating a star. What happens next depends on how massive the star is.

Nebula
Protostars begin to form from gas inside a nebula. Once a star is big enough, nuclear fusion begins inside it. Hydrogen is converted to helium, making the star shine.

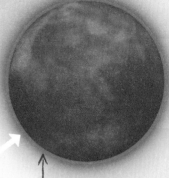

Main sequence
Protostars become main-sequence stars and enter a long stable phase. This continues until all the hydrogen in the core has been used up.

Red supergiant
If the star has a large mass, it expands and cools, becoming red and forming a red supergiant star.

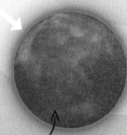

Red giant
If the star has less mass, it expands, cools, and becomes red to form a red giant. Our Sun will follow this path.

DRAW THE STAR MEMORIES

Can you complete this star's life story from birth to its final destiny? You'll need to read the captions carefully to know which kind of star it is, then draw each moment in the white boxes above.

a Aw, look at me in the star nursery—just a cute cloud of dust and gas.

b My main-sequence years, when I fused into a massive star.

c Wow, look how much I've grown— I'm a supergiant!

d BOOM! This is when I ran out of fuel and exploded!

e Here I am now— spinning and shining like a celestial lighthouse.

 DRAW IT!

Neutron star
If the core remaining after the supernova has little mass, it becomes a dense, spinning neutron star.

Black hole
If the core remaining after the supernova has a larger mass, it forms a black hole—an area with such strong gravity that everything is pulled into it, even light.

Supernova
Eventually, the supergiant explodes, becoming a supernova.

White dwarf
Once fusion stops and the star runs out of fuel, it sheds its outer layers and the core collapses into a white dwarf.

Black dwarf
Finally, after billions of years, the white dwarf cools and stops glowing, becoming a black dwarf.

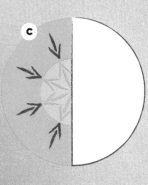

THE CLOSEST **BLACK HOLE** TO THE SUN IS ABOUT **1,560** LIGHT-YEARS AWAY, IN THE SYSTEM **GAIA BH1.**

WHAT'S IT CALLED?
When a supergiant collapses, it can create an area of space so dense that not even light can escape. What is the name of this strange space object? Unscramble the letters below to find out.

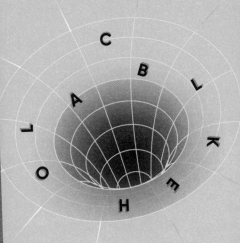

FIND THE BALANCE
When the fuel inside stars begins to run out, the balance between their gravity and the energy they create shifts. This is when stars become unbalanced and move to the next stage in their life cycle. These diagrams show the balance of forces at different stages in a star's life. Can you match them to the correct descriptions, then draw in the other half to match?

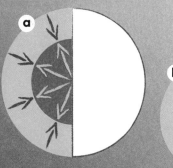

Normal star
The star is balanced, with the inward pull of its gravity matched by outward pressure from the energy in its core.

Red giant
As the star gets older, its core heats up, releasing more energy and pushing out against its gravity.

Black hole
Once a massive star runs out of fuel, it no longer releases energy and its gravity forces the star to collapse.

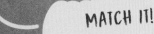

MATCH IT!

EXOPLANETS

Planets that orbit stars other than our Sun are known as exoplanets. So far, scientists have detected more than 5,000 exoplanets spread across nearly 4,000 different planetary systems. Many more potential exoplanets are currently being investigated.

THERE COULD BE AS MANY AS **300 MILLION** HABITABLE PLANETS IN OUR **GALAXY.**

Gas giants
These planets start at the size of Saturn or Jupiter, but they can be much larger. Some of them travel in very close, hot orbits around their stars.

Neptune-like
These planets are a similar size to Neptune and Uranus. They are thought to have a rocky core and an atmosphere of hydrogen gas.

Super-Earth
Typically, rocky planets that are more massive than Earth but lighter than Neptune.

Terrestrial
Planets made of rock and metal, which are a similar size to Earth or smaller.

FIND A NEW HOME
The search for life on other planets starts by working out which planets have just the right conditions. Look at the checklist below, then circle the planet you think could provide a home where humans could safely and comfortably live.

Checklist:
- ☐ Liquid water present
- ☐ Solid surface
- ☐ 32°F–212°F (0°C–100°C)
- ☐ Relatively small

CIRCLE IT!

77°F (25°C)
572°F (300°C)
−508°F (−300°C)
59°F (15°C)
−184°F (−120°C)

A
B
C
D
E

Key
- (A) Gas giant, water in ice form
- (B) Gas giant, liquid water
- (C) Rocky planet, vaporized water
- (D) Rocky planet, liquid water
- (E) Rocky planet, water in ice form

SORT THE SYSTEMS

The universe is home to many planetary systems: a group of planets centered around one or more stars. Can you match each of these planetary systems to the correct description?

GJ 357

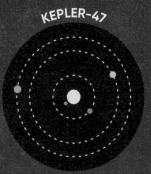
KEPLER-47

KEPLER-62

MATCH IT!

Sun-like
Five planets surround this star, which is similar to our Sun but a little fainter.

Super-Earth
This red dwarf star is orbited by three planets, including a super-Earth.

Pair of stars
Three planets orbit this binary star (two stars that orbit each other).

PUT EACH PLANET IN A BOX

It's time to find out how much you've learned about exoplanets. Read about each planet below and work out what type of exoplanet it is. Then draw it in the box under the correct type shown above.

	TERRESTRIAL	SUPER-EARTH	NEPTUNE-LIKE	GAS GIANT
Planet A Same size as Uranus. Hydrogen gas in its atmosphere.				
Planet B Half the size of Earth. Made of rock and metal.				
Planet C Rocky. Five times more massive than Earth. Smaller than Neptune.				
Planet D Very big. Made of gas. Very hot. Orbits close to its star.				

DRAW IT!

NEBULAS

The universe is scattered with enormous areas of dust and gas called nebulas. They often appear as colorful, glowing clouds. Some nebulas have new stars being born within them, while others form only as stars die.

SOME **NEBULAS** ARE CALLED **"STELLAR NURSERIES"** BECAUSE THEY CONTAIN **BABY STARS.**

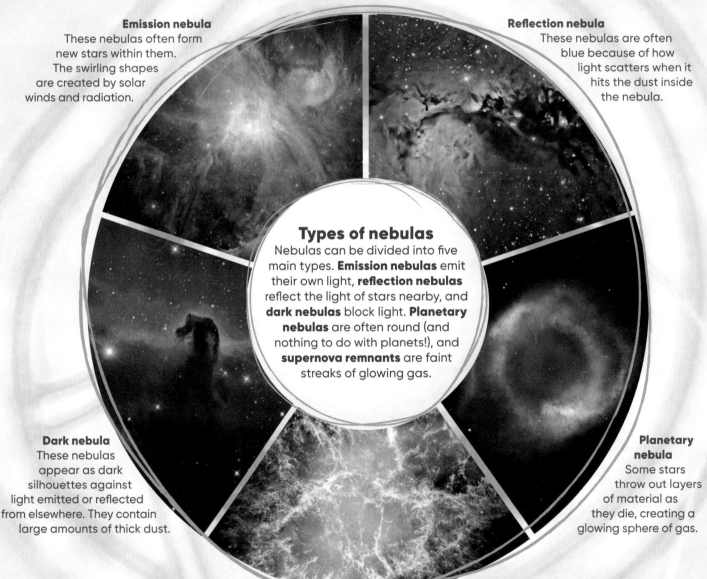

Emission nebula
These nebulas often form new stars within them. The swirling shapes are created by solar winds and radiation.

Reflection nebula
These nebulas are often blue because of how light scatters when it hits the dust inside the nebula.

Types of nebulas
Nebulas can be divided into five main types. **Emission nebulas** emit their own light, **reflection nebulas** reflect the light of stars nearby, and **dark nebulas** block light. **Planetary nebulas** are often round (and nothing to do with planets!), and **supernova remnants** are faint streaks of glowing gas.

Dark nebula
These nebulas appear as dark silhouettes against light emitted or reflected from elsewhere. They contain large amounts of thick dust.

Planetary nebula
Some stars throw out layers of material as they die, creating a glowing sphere of gas.

Supernova remnants
When a massive star dies, it can explode into a supernova. This type of nebula is what remains after a supernova.

WHAT CAN YOU SEE?

Nebulas can be seen from Earth, but the best, up-close images of them are taken by the Hubble Space Telescope. Can you match each of these pictures to the correct viewpoint? They all show the Orion Nebula.

MATCH IT!

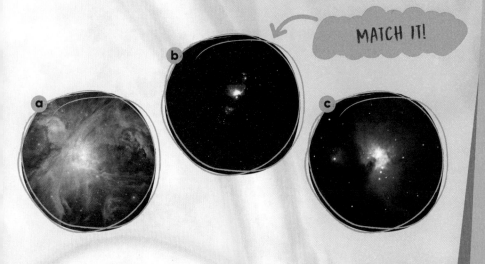

a

b

c

Naked eye
This is what we can see from Earth, with no magnifying equipment.

Zooming in
This photo was taken from Earth with a magnifying camera and a long exposure.

Close-up
This image was taken by the Hubble Space Telescope.

CREATE YOUR OWN NEBULA
Two of the most distinctive nebulas are the Horsehead Nebula and the Butterfly Nebula. Use this space to design your own nebula in the shape of your favorite animal, then give it a name.

DRAW IT!

Butterfly Nebula

Horsehead Nebula

....

Galaxy shapes

Galaxies are usually grouped into four types, depending on how they appear. The most common type is spiral.

Spiral
Curved arms spiral out from a central disk. Older stars are in the center, newer stars on the arms.

Barred spiral
Similar to spiral, but with a straight bar across the middle. The Milky Way is a barred spiral.

Elliptical
A squashed ball shape. These galaxies mostly contain very old, dim stars.

Irregular
Stars aren't arranged in any particular shape. These galaxies are usually quite small.

GALAXIES

Most stars aren't alone in space—gravity holds billions of them together in groups called galaxies. Galaxies are enormous. Along with stars, they contain any planets that orbit the stars plus asteroids, dust, and gas.

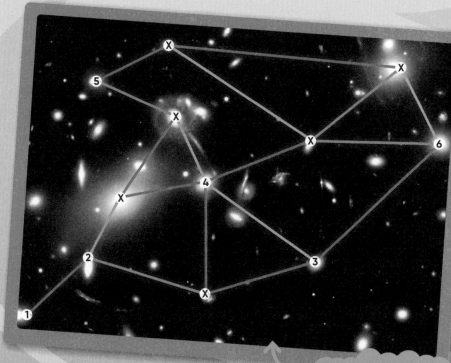

FIND IT!

CROSS THE CLUSTER GALAXY

Make your way across this cluster of galaxies (above) by the quickest route. Each route takes a different amount of time, and you must visit each numbered galaxy in order from 1 to 6.

Key

— 1 million light-years

— 2 million light-years

— 3 million light-years

How long did it take?

....

....

THERE ARE AROUND **200 BILLION** GALAXIES IN THE PARTS OF THE UNIVERSE **WE CAN SEE.**

WHICH SHAPE IS WHICH?

Here are four galaxies, one of each shape. Use the information on these pages to help you label them.

a ....

b ....

d ....

c ....

WRITE IT!

SOLVE THE GALAXY-DOKU

Complete this grid by drawing in galaxies. Each galaxy shape should appear only once in each column; row; and smaller, four-square grid.

Key

 Spiral

 Elliptical

 Barred spiral

 Irregular

REVEAL THE GALAXY

What type is the galaxy hidden in this cloud of dots? Starting in the middle, draw a line to each star of the same color one by one until the galaxy is revealed.

DRAW IT!

+
START HERE

BONUS QUESTION
What type is our galaxy?

....

THE MILKY WAY

Our galaxy, the Milky Way, is just one of the trillions of galaxies in the universe. It is a collection of stars, gas, and dust held together by gravity.

Our galaxy

The Milky Way is a barred spiral galaxy around 90,000 light-years wide, with a number of arms curving out from a central bulge and bar. There are two main arms: the Perseus Arm and Scutum-Centaurus Arm.

Around 10 billion of the galaxy's stars are grouped in a bulge in the center.

THE NORMA ARM

THE ORION ARM

At the center of the Milky Way is a supermassive black hole called Sagittarius A*.

The Sun and our Solar System are here, in a partial arm called the Orion Arm.

NAME THAT ARM!

Here, the names of some of the arms of the Milky Way have got jumbled up. Rearrange the letters and write the names below.

R O N O I

a _ _ _ _ _ Arm

E S P U E R S

b _ _ _ _ _ _ _ Arm

M A N O R

c _ _ _ _ _ Arm

I T S A T S G A U R I

d _ _ _ _ _ _ _ _ _ _ _ Arm

LABEL THE GALAXY

Viewed from the side, the Milky Way has a bulge at its center surrounded by a thinner main disk, which contains the arms. Use the word box to help you write the missing labels onto this diagram.

Central bulge   Main disk

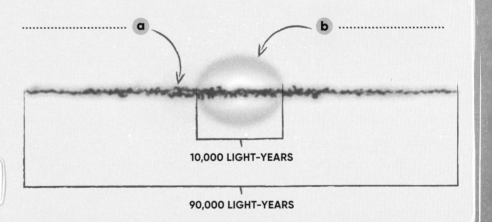

a

b

10,000 LIGHT-YEARS

90,000 LIGHT-YEARS

THE SCUTUM-CENTAURUS ARM

THE SAGITTARIUS ARM

THE PERSEUS ARM

FIND IT!

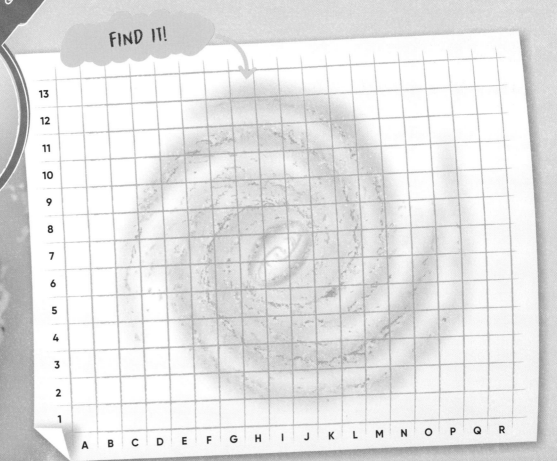

BUILD THE MILKY WAY
Follow the steps below to help you complete this picture of the Milky Way.

1. Color the gray spiraling arms, using the main image on these pages for guidance.

2. Plot the coordinates given in the key on the right and write a label pointing to each location.

Key
✕ Sagittarius Arm (M,10)
✕ Perseus Arm (N,4)
✕ Sagittarius A* (I,7)
✕ Our Sun (H,4)
✕ Scutum-Centaurus Arm (F,11)
✕ Norma Arm (E,7)

DRAW IT!

DRAW THE VIEW
From Earth, the Milky Way appears as a hazy band of milky-colored light curving across the night sky. Draw the place you live along the bottom, then draw the Milky Way across the sky.

The Milky Way, as seen from Earth

LOOKING UP

People have studied the night sky for thousands of years. The Moon and stars are very familiar to us, but there are plenty of other, less obvious things to look for, too. Studying these objects teaches us about our universe and Earth's place in it. In fact, this is a whole branch of science called astronomy.

The celestial sphere

Astronomers map the night sky using an imaginary sphere around our planet called the celestial sphere. What you can see depends on where you are on Earth and changes as Earth turns on its axis and moves around the Sun.

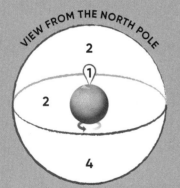

SCIENTISTS WHO STUDY THE **UNIVERSE** ARE CALLED **COSMOLOGISTS.**

The north celestial pole, above Earth's North Pole

THE CELESTIAL SPHERE

THE SUN

The celestial equator, which lines up with Earth's equator

COLOR THE SPHERES

Because Earth spins as it orbits the Sun, different parts of the celestial sphere come into view during the year. The visible area also depends where on Earth you are. Color these diagrams to show how much can be seen from these three places in a year.

Coloring key

1 Observer
2 Stars always visible
3 Stars sometimes visible
4 Stars never visible

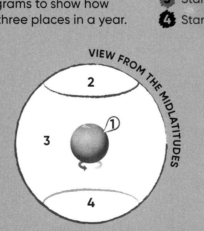

VIEW FROM THE NORTH POLE

2

1

2

4

VIEW FROM THE MIDLATITUDES

2

1

3

4

VIEW FROM THE EQUATOR

3

1

COLOR IT!

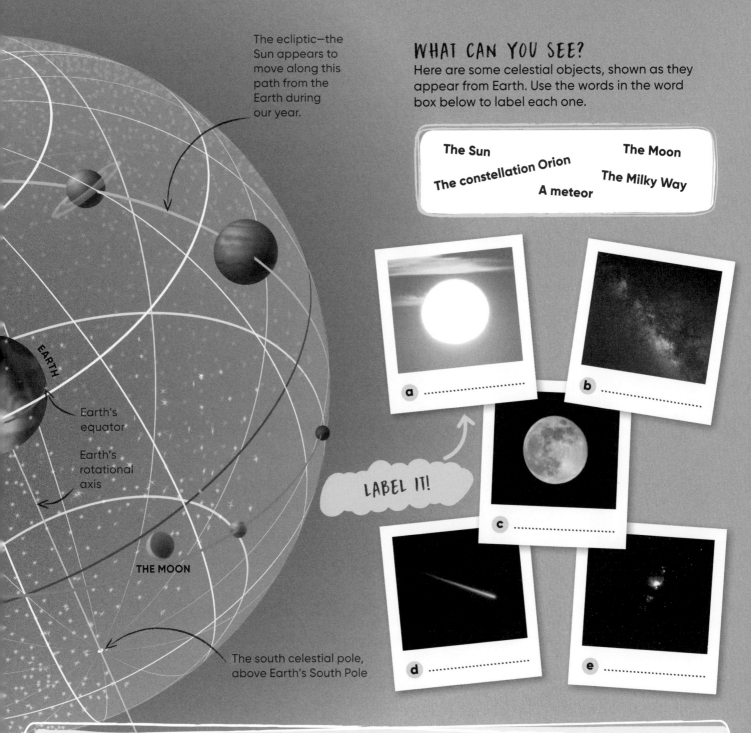

The ecliptic—the Sun appears to move along this path from the Earth during our year.

EARTH

Earth's equator

Earth's rotational axis

THE MOON

The south celestial pole, above Earth's South Pole

WHAT CAN YOU SEE?

Here are some celestial objects, shown as they appear from Earth. Use the words in the word box below to label each one.

The Sun   **The Moon**

The constellation Orion   **The Milky Way**

A meteor

LABEL IT!

a ....

b ....

c ....

d ....

e ....

NAME THE SYSTEM

Early astronomers believed that Earth was the center of the universe, with the Sun, Moon, planets, and stars orbiting around us. This is called a **"geocentric"** system. In 1543, an astronomer named Nicolaus Copernicus suggested a **"heliocentric"** system, with the Sun at the center of the Solar System and Earth and the planets orbiting around it. This is the model we now know to be correct. Label these diagrams to indicate which system they each show.

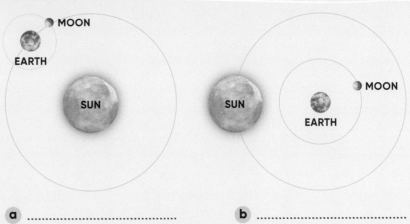

MOON

EARTH

SUN

SUN

MOON

EARTH

a ....   b ....

CONSTELLATIONS

For thousands of years, people have studied the night sky and looked for patterns in the stars. These patterns of stars are called constellations. They are named after characters from ancient stories, animals, and objects. Small groups of stars within constellations are called asterisms.

Star shapes
Constellations are imaginary patterns seen by humans. People in different cultures have seen different patterns in the same set of stars over time.

The Western zodiac
As Earth travels around the Sun, the Sun appears to follow a path across the night sky, which is known as the ecliptic. Only 13 constellations lie on the ecliptic. They are known as the constellations of the zodiac.

Key
— Celestial equator
  Ecliptic

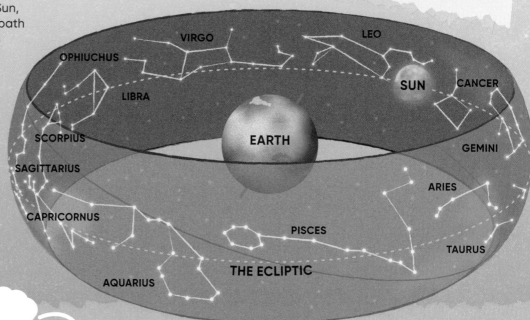

VIRGO · LEO · OPHIUCHUS · SUN · CANCER · LIBRA · SCORPIUS · EARTH · GEMINI · SAGITTARIUS · ARIES · CAPRICORNUS · PISCES · TAURUS · AQUARIUS · THE ECLIPTIC

MATCH IT!

MATCH THE STORIES
Here are some well-known constellations, which have been separated from their stories. Read the stories, match them to the correct constellations above, then write in their names.

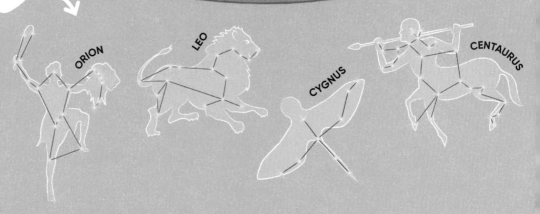

ORION · LEO · CYGNUS · CENTAURUS

WRITE IT!

a ....
This constellation was said to be the lion killed by Hercules, a hero of Greek mythology.

b ....
This constellation represents a centaur, a mythical creature that was half man and half horse.

c ....
A great hunter, shown raising his club in the air. A line of three bright stars forms his belt.

d ....
Named after the Latin word for swan, this constellation looks like a bird in flight.

DESIGN YOUR OWN CONSTELLATIONS

Draw lines to connect stars together and create your own constellations. Why not try drawing animals, objects, or people?

DRAW IT!

OVER THOUSANDS OF YEARS, **STARS MOVE** AND CONSTELLATIONS **CHANGE** SHAPE.

HOW FAR?

Stars in constellations appear to be next to each other, but they are actually scattered across space. Use the colors in the key to complete this diagram showing the distances between the stars in the constellation Orion.

Coloring key

- **Betelgeuse** 498 light-years
- **Bellatrix** 243 light-years
- **Rigel** 850 light-years
- **Alnitak** 736 light-years
- **Mintaka** 691 light-years

COLOR IT!

DISTANCE IN LIGHT-YEARS

0   100   200   300   400   500   600   700   800   900

COMPLETE THE CONSTELLATIONS

The constellations below and on the far right are missing their lines. Find the matching section of sky on the star charts, then copy the lines to complete each constellation.

STAR MAPS

Star charts are maps of the night sky that show where stars and constellations will appear. As Earth rotates and moves around the Sun, the constellations appear to move. We see different constellations depending on where we are and what time of year it is.

COMPLETE IT!

NORTHERN SKY

The northern hemisphere
Northern skies are centered around Polaris, the North Star. This star is always visible in the northern hemisphere—it never sets below the horizon.

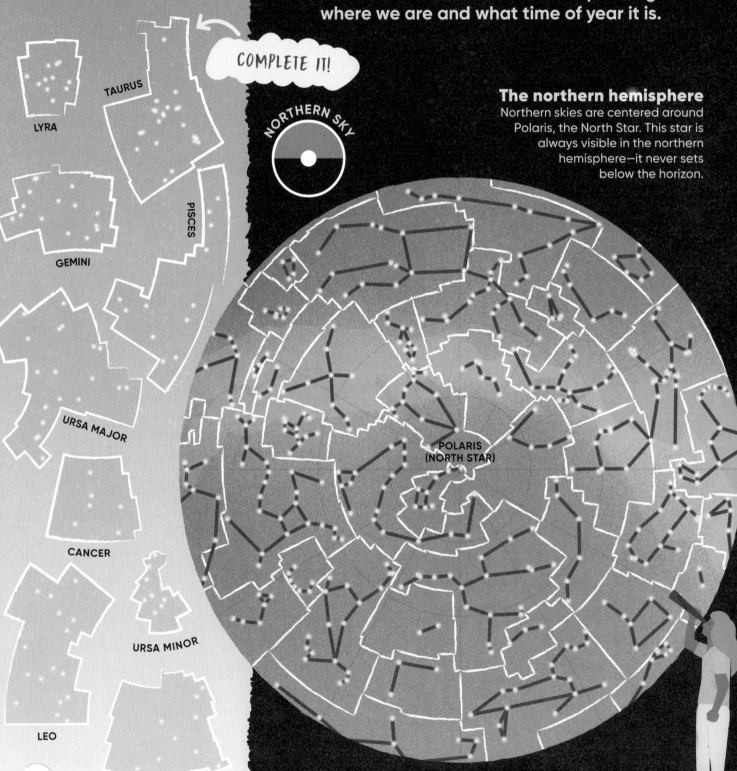

LYRA

TAURUS

PISCES

GEMINI

URSA MAJOR

CANCER

URSA MINOR

LEO

CYGNUS

POLARIS
(NORTH STAR)

North and south

To map the stars, we imagine a colossal sphere around Earth. This sphere is split into two hemispheres, north and south, along a line that corresponds to Earth's equator. Each hemisphere is divided into smaller sections of sky, with a constellation in each of them.

NORTHERN HEMISPHERE

Earth's equator

SOUTHERN HEMISPHERE

The southern hemisphere

The southern skies do not have one single bright star to mark the center. However, there are many bright constellations here, including Crux (the Southern Cross).

SOUTHERN SKY

CANIS MAJOR

INDUS

SAGITTARIUS

FORNAX

CENTAURUS

LUPUS

LEPUS

HYDRUS

PUPPIS

OUR SKIES ARE DIVIDED INTO **88** CONSTELLATIONS.

TELESCOPES

We can't see far into space with just our eyes.
Telescopes offer a magnified view, letting us see
much farther and in more detail than we can without
them. They come in a range of sizes and powers,
from amateur telescopes you can hold in your
hand to colossal space telescopes that orbit Earth.

THE
BIGGEST
TELESCOPES COLLECT
100 MILLION
TIMES MORE LIGHT
THAN THE NAKED EYE.

Inside a telescope
Telescopes collect light and
focus it, creating an image.
Simple telescopes do this using
either refraction or reflection.

Main lens

LIGHT FROM OBJECT

Eyepiece

Refracting telescope
These telescopes collect
light using lenses. The main
lens collects the light and
bends (refracts) it, creating an
image. Another lens, called the
eyepiece, makes the image bigger.

LIGHT FROM OBJECT

Eyepiece

Second
mirror

Reflecting telescope
These telescopes use
mirrors to collect light.
The main mirror collects and
focuses light, then reflects it
toward a second mirror.
The second mirror bounces
the light into the eyepiece lens.

Main mirror

REFLECT OR REFRACT?
These two diagrams have had
the light rays removed. Use the
information in the panel above
to help you label whether it is
a **refracting** telescope or a
reflecting telescope. Then
draw in the paths that light
takes through each of them.

DRAW IT!

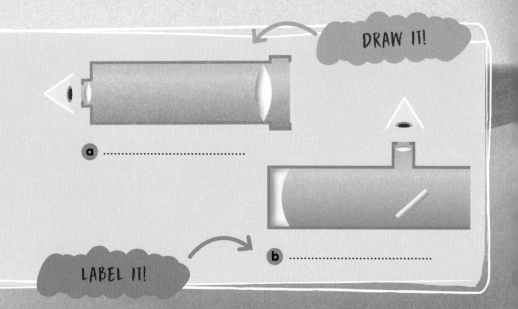

a ....

b ....

LABEL IT!

60

WHAT CAN YOU SEE?

Earth-based telescopes can be blocked by clouds or dust in the atmosphere. To get around this, astronomers send telescopes such as the Hubble Space Telescope into space. Can you circle the eight differences between these two pictures of Hubble?

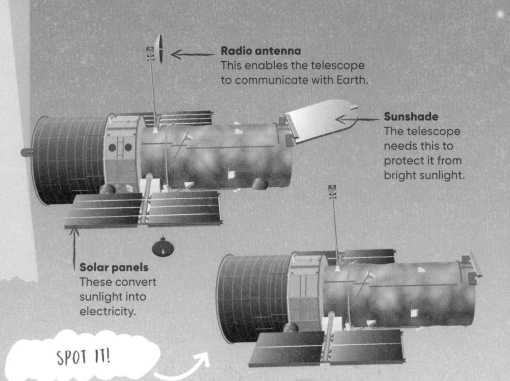

Radio antenna
This enables the telescope to communicate with Earth.

Sunshade
The telescope needs this to protect it from bright sunlight.

Solar panels
These convert sunlight into electricity.

SPOT IT!

VERY LARGE TELESCOPE

LOCATION: _Cerro Paranal, Chile_

ALTITUDE: _8,645 feet (2,635 m)_

SIZE OF MAIN MIRROR: ....

KECK TELESCOPES

LOCATION: ....

ALTITUDE: _13,600 feet (4,145 m)_

SIZE OF MAIN MIRROR: _33 feet (10 m)_

GRAN TELESCOPIO CANARIAS

LOCATION: _La Palma, Canary Islands_

ALTITUDE: ....

SIZE OF MAIN MIRROR: _34 feet (10.4 m)_

COMPLETE THE FACT FILES

To study space from Earth, astronomers use observatories—buildings containing astronomical telescopes that collect light using enormous mirrors. Observatories are often built high up, where there is less light pollution. Use the words in the box to help you complete these fact files about some famous observatories.

Mauna Kea, Hawaii

7,440 feet (2,267 m)   27 feet (8.2 m)

Timeline of the Space Age

One of the first objects sent into space was a satellite that sent radio signals. Since then, spacecrafts have become much more advanced, able to travel far into space and even to carry people. This timeline shows a few key events in our space history.

 First video game invented, NASA founded

 The LED light invented

1957
Sputnik becomes the first human-made satellite sent into space.

1959
Luna 3 takes the first pictures of the far side of the Moon.

1961
Yuri Gagarin is the first human in space.

1963
Valentina Tereshkova becomes the first woman in space.

1965
The first spacewalk is made by Alexei Leonov.

WHO WENT FIRST?

Who was the first person to travel into space? Unscramble the letters below to spell out the answer.

_ _ _ _   _ _ _ _ _ _ _

N G A I A I R
 R Y U G

MORE THAN
500 PEOPLE
HAVE TRAVELED INTO **SPACE.**

SPACE EXPLORATION

Humans have looked up into space for millions of years, but spacecrafts have only been around since the second half of the 20th century. Over time, more complex and innovative technologies have allowed us to explore farther into the Solar System and even beyond it.

WHAT HAPPENED WHEN?

Here are some images of key people and events in space history. Use the information in the timeline above to help you write in the missing dates.

 SPUTNIK LAUNCHED

1ST MAN IN SPACE

1ST WOMAN IN SPACE

THE MOON LANDING

1ST ISS MODULE LAUNCHED

a _ _ _ _ _   **b** _ _ _ _ _   **c** _ _ _ _ _   **d** _ _ _ _ _   **e** _ _ _ _ _

WRITE IT!

1969
Neil Armstrong
becomes the first
person to walk
on the Moon.

1971
Salyut 1 becomes
the world's first
space station.

1977
The *Voyager*
missions launch,
heading for the
edge of the Solar
System.

1990
The Hubble
Space Telescope
is launched.

1998
The first
module of the
International
Space Station
is launched.

2014
Philae becomes
the first lander
to touch down
on a comet.

MATCH THE ANIMALS

Before people visited space, animals went first.
Scientists studied the animals to see how their
bodies coped with zero gravity. Match these
famous space travelers to their descriptions
and write their names on the photos.

a ....

b ....

c ....

DESIGN A MARS SPACESUIT

Humans haven't visited Mars yet, but it's on the
list. With average temperatures of –76°F (–60°C)
and no oxygen, we wouldn't last longer than
a minute without a spacesuit. Can you design
one? Here are some things you could include:

1. A strong but flexible suit (to keep you warm and
protect you from solar radiation while still allowing
you to move around easily), with a helmet and visor
to keep breathable air in and block bright sunlight.

2. A backpack containing oxygen, water, batteries,
and a radio (to talk to the other astronauts).

Tardigrades
In 2008, the European Space
Agency (ESA) discovered
that these tiny "water bears"
could survive in open space.

Belka and Strelka
These two dogs were the
first animals to complete
an orbit of our planet and
return home, in 1960.

Ham
As a final rehearsal before the first
human flight, this chimpanzee was
launched into space in 1961 and
coped well with the mission.

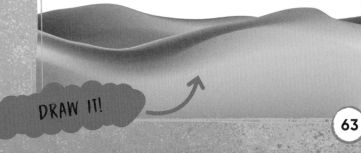

DRAW IT!

ROCKETS

Breaking free of Earth's gravity requires a colossal amount of energy. So far, the only vehicles we have invented that can do this are rockets. Rockets carry huge amounts of fuel to create the necessary thrust. Most of them are designed to fly into space only once and cannot be reused.

How rockets work

Rockets carry huge tanks of fuel, as well as liquid oxygen, which is needed to make the fuel burn. The fuel and oxygen are mixed together and lit, forming a reaction that forces hot gases out of the rocket's exhaust. The push of the exhaust gases lifts the rocket up and away from the ground.

LIQUID OXYGEN

FUEL

THRUST

Pumps

Combustion chamber

Nozzle

Hot exhaust gases

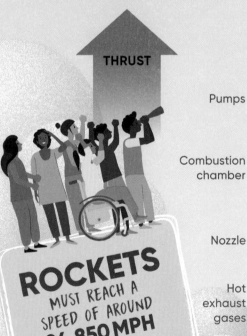

ROCKETS
MUST REACH A SPEED OF AROUND **24,850 MPH** (40,000 KPH) **TO BREAK OUT** OF EARTH'S GRAVITY.

COMPLETE THE ROCKET
Use all the information on this page to help you complete the diagram below.

1. Choose two colors to complete the key and use them to color the rocket.

2. Label the diagram, using the words from the illustration on the left.

COLOR IT!

Coloring key
- Fuel
- Liquid oxygen

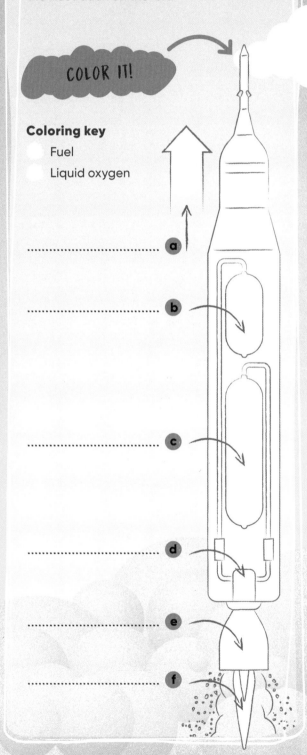

.... **a**

.... **b**

.... **c**

.... **d**

.... **e**

.... **f**

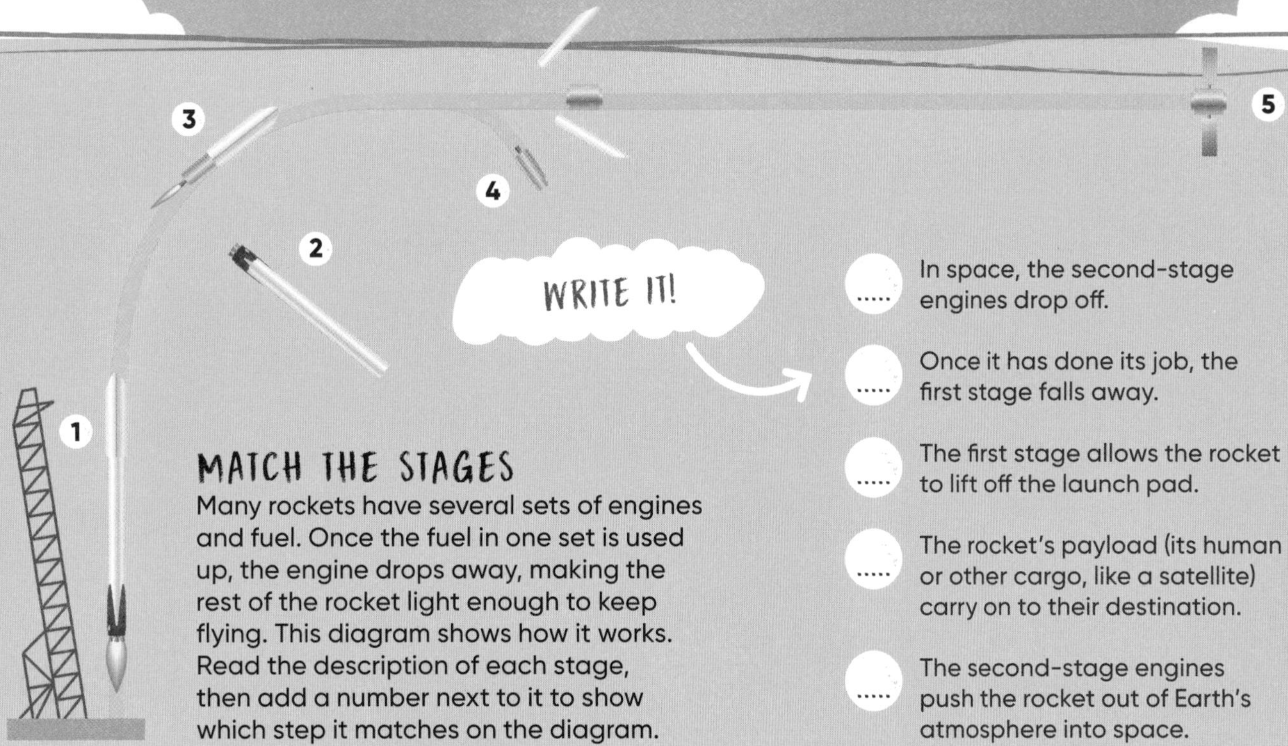

3

5

4

2

1

WRITE IT!

MATCH THE STAGES

Many rockets have several sets of engines and fuel. Once the fuel in one set is used up, the engine drops away, making the rest of the rocket light enough to keep flying. This diagram shows how it works. Read the description of each stage, then add a number next to it to show which step it matches on the diagram.

..... In space, the second-stage engines drop off.

..... Once it has done its job, the first stage falls away.

..... The first stage allows the rocket to lift off the launch pad.

..... The rocket's payload (its human or other cargo, like a satellite) carry on to their destination.

..... The second-stage engines push the rocket out of Earth's atmosphere into space.

AROUND
TWO ROCKETS
LAUNCH INTO SPACE
FROM EARTH
EVERY WEEK.

5, 4, 3, 2, 1...

FIND THE NAME
What is the term used to describe a rocket taking off? Unscramble the letters below.

F I T F O L F

_ _ _ _ _ _

ENOUGH THRUST?
Rockets are pushed upward by a force called thrust. To reach orbit, a rocket must have enough thrust to overcome the downward force of Earth's gravity (weight). Look at the arrows beside these rockets—green shows gravity and red shows thrust. Color the triangles beneath the rockets to show which ones will reach orbit.

Key
▲ Thrust wins!
▼ Gravity wins!

a △▽   b △▽   c △▽   d △▽   e △▽

SPACE PROBES

Humans can't travel very far into space—it is dangerous, and the distances are incredibly long. Instead, we send robotic spacecrafts known as probes to explore the planets and objects that make up our Solar System. Each probe carries scientific instruments to collect data and send it back to Earth.

THE FIRST EVER **PROBE** WAS THE SOVIET UNION'S **SPUTNIK** LAUNCHED ON **OCTOBER 4, 1957.**

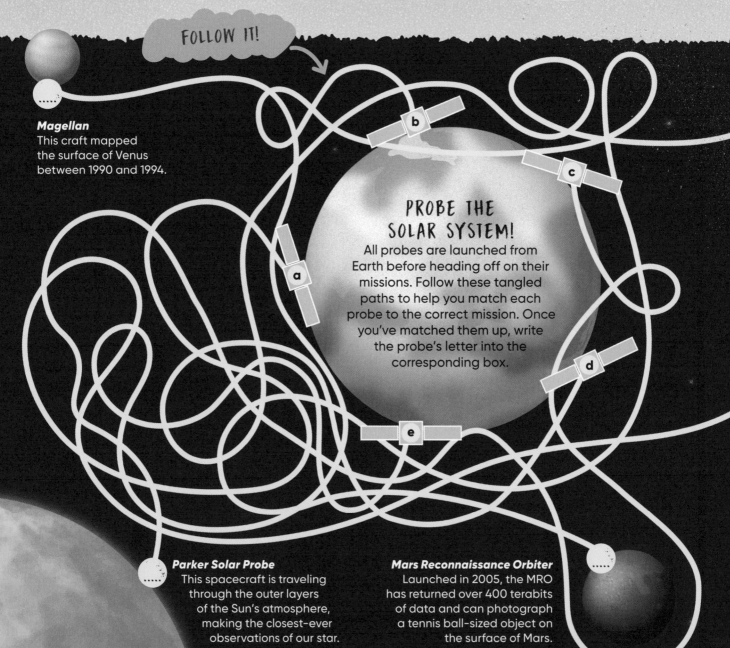

FOLLOW IT!

Magellan
This craft mapped the surface of Venus between 1990 and 1994.

PROBE THE SOLAR SYSTEM!
All probes are launched from Earth before heading off on their missions. Follow these tangled paths to help you match each probe to the correct mission. Once you've matched them up, write the probe's letter into the corresponding box.

Parker Solar Probe
This spacecraft is traveling through the outer layers of the Sun's atmosphere, making the closest-ever observations of our star.

Mars Reconnaissance Orbiter
Launched in 2005, the MRO has returned over 400 terabits of data and can photograph a tennis ball-sized object on the surface of Mars.

Types of probes
There are four main types of space probes:

Orbiter

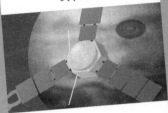

Orbiter probes go into orbit around their target space object, making detailed studies from high above the surface.

Flyby

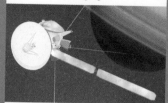

These probes fly past their target, far enough away that they aren't captured by the object's gravity. This is a good way to find out basic information.

Lander

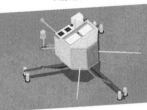

These probes land on the surface of their target. Once down, they collect soil and rock samples and observe weather conditions.

Rover

These crafts have wheels to travel around the surface of their target, exploring it in great detail, sometimes for years.

Cassini-Huygens
The *Cassini* spacecraft orbited Saturn, then dropped the *Huygens* lander down to Titan, Saturn's largest moon.

Pioneer 10
The first probe to cross the Asteroid Belt and reach Jupiter. In 1983, it left the Solar System.

MATCH IT!

MATCH AND IDENTIFY

Read about each of these missions; match them to the correct image; then fill in the labels to say whether the spacecraft was a **flyby**, **orbiter**, **lander**, or **rover**.

WRITE IT!

a.

b.

c.

d.

OSIRIS-REx
This craft touched down on the surface of asteroid Bennu and collected a dust sample.

New Horizons
This probe flew past the dwarf planet Pluto in 2015. The journey to get there took nine years.

Opportunity
This vehicle explored the surface of Mars from 2004 to 2018. It was searching for signs of water.

Juno
This probe is in close orbit around Jupiter. It is powered by three highly efficient solar panels.

....

ROVERS

Originally designed to explore the surface of the Moon, rovers are spacecrafts packed with scientific equipment and programmed to find their own way around. Rovers have been exploring Mars since *Sojourner* touched down in 1997. They use radio signals to communicate with Earth.

IT CAN TAKE **20 MINUTES** FOR A MESSAGE **SENT BY A ROVER** ON MARS TO REACH EARTH.

Perseverance rover

NASA's *Perseverance* rover is the largest and most advanced rover to visit Mars so far. It has been exploring the planet's surface since 2021, taking rock samples and looking for signs of ancient life.

The rover has 23 cameras, including a high-resolution "SuperCam."

A drill on the robotic arm allows the craft to extract rock core samples.

Six aluminum wheels and titanium "legs" keep the rover steady and allow it to drive over rough, uneven ground and obstacles.

A set of sensors measure atmospheric pressure, temperature, humidity, and winds.

MARTIAN VIEWS

Rovers have taken some incredible photographs of the surface of Mars. Can you draw lines to match each of these images to the correct description?

Curiosity

Opportunity

Perseverance

Sojourner

MATCH IT!

a This rover found a mass of tiny spheres of rock. They became known as "Martian blueberries."

b This image of rolling, rocky Martian hills is a composite of seven images taken in 1997 by this rover.

c This photo shows the tracks left on a Martian dune by the rover that took the photograph.

d This photo is of *Ingenuity*, a helicopter drone that is on a Mars mission with this rover.

COMPLETE THE FACT FILES

Some information is missing from these profiles of three rovers that have explored Mars. Use the word box to help you complete them.

July 23, 2020	NASA	December 4, 1996
Gale Crater	25.4 lb (11.5 kg)	May 14, 2021

SOJOURNER

AGENCY:	NASA
WEIGHT OF ROVER:	....
DATE LAUNCHED:	....
DATE OF ARRIVAL:	July 4, 1997
LANDING SITE:	Ares Vallis
MISSION: (COMPLETED)	To prove that a rover could be sent to Mars

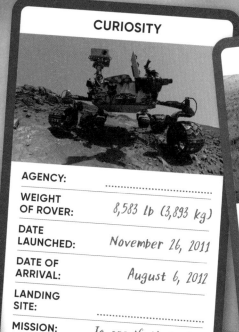

CURIOSITY

AGENCY:	....
WEIGHT OF ROVER:	8,583 lb (3,893 kg)
DATE LAUNCHED:	November 26, 2011
DATE OF ARRIVAL:	August 6, 2012
LANDING SITE:	....
MISSION: (ONGOING)	To see if there has been life on Mars

ZHURONG

AGENCY:	CNSA
WEIGHT OF ROVER:	529 lb (240 kg)
DATE LAUNCHED:	....
DATE OF ARRIVAL:	....
LANDING SITE:	Utopia Planitia
MISSION: (ONGOING)	To detect water below the planet's surface

DRAW IT!

DESIGN YOUR OWN ROVER

Can you invent a new kind of rover to investigate Mars? Draw your design here. The rover needs to be able to complete these jobs:

1. It must climb steep slopes and cross rough, uneven ground without falling.

2. It will need cameras, drills, and scientific instruments to analyze the soil and rocks.

3. It must be able to communicate with scientists on Earth.

CREWED SPACECRAFTS

In the 1960s, scientists developed spacecrafts that were able to carry astronauts into space. At first, these crafts were tiny, carrying just one person for a short time. Eventually, they became more advanced, able to carry several people for longer missions. So far, only three nations have launched crewed spacecrafts: the US, Russia, and China.

Space transport

Russian cosmonauts currently travel to the International Space Station (ISS) in a *Soyuz* craft. *Soyuz* can carry up to three people at a time. It has three modules—the orbital module, descent module, and service module—and is launched into space in the nose of a *Soyuz FG* rocket.

The service module contains the engines and fuel. It is a noncrew area.

The descent module is the only part that will return to Earth. It is designed to keep the astronauts safe as the craft descends to Earth.

The orbital module is where the crew live and work while they are on board the craft.

The hatch can be opened to allow astronauts to and from the ISS.

JOURNEY INTO SPACE AND BACK

This diagram shows the stages in the *Soyuz* craft's journey to and from the ISS. Read the descriptions of each stage below, then color the arrows in the diagram.

COLOR IT!

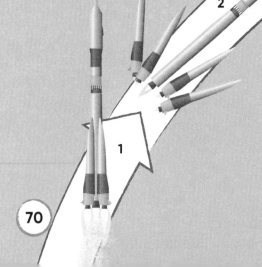

Coloring key

1 A rocket lifts off, carrying *Soyuz* up and away from Earth.

2 Rocket boosters use up their fuel, then fall away from the craft.

3 The main fuel tank empties and falls away.

4 The second-stage fuel tank falls away.

5 *Soyuz* docks with the ISS.

6 *Soyuz* detaches itself from the ISS.

7 The orbital and service modules separate off from the descent module.

8 Parachutes open to slow the descent module's fall through Earth's atmosphere.

9 Two small engines fire upward to soften the module's landing.

WHICH CRAFT IS WHICH?

Here are a number of crewed spacecrafts, which have been separated from their descriptions. First, connect the dots. Then draw lines to match up the correct pairs.

MATCH IT!

DRAW IT!

Space shuttle
Five space shuttles operated during the craft's lifetime. They could carry crews of up to eight people.

SpaceX *Crew Dragon*
This reusable craft will carry future crews to the ISS and back, touching back down on its four landing legs.

SpaceShipTwo
This planelike spacecraft has been designed for private space tourism.

Gemini
This compact, conical craft carried the two-man team who made the first US spacewalk.

SOYUZ
SPACECRAFTS HAVE BEEN CARRYING PEOPLE INTO SPACE FOR MORE THAN 50 YEARS.

Space crew landing
When *Soyuz* crafts return to Earth, they drift down on parachutes and hit the ground with a bump. Once the craft has landed, the crew are helped out of the capsule by a search and rescue team. *Soyuz* crafts always land back in Kazakhstan, near the Russian Baikonur Cosmodrome spaceport.

LABEL THE SPACECRAFT

Use the information in the panels and the words in the box to help you label this diagram of *Apollo 11* and *Saturn V*.

Command module   Third stage

First stage   Second stage

Service module   Lunar module

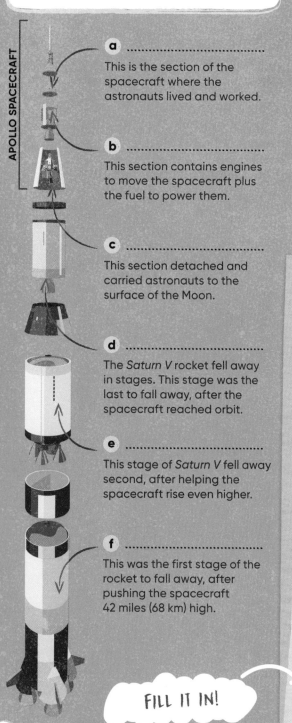

APOLLO SPACECRAFT

a ....
This is the section of the spacecraft where the astronauts lived and worked.

b ....
This section contains engines to move the spacecraft plus the fuel to power them.

c ....
This section detached and carried astronauts to the surface of the Moon.

d ....
The *Saturn V* rocket fell away in stages. This stage was the last to fall away, after the spacecraft reached orbit.

e ....
This stage of *Saturn V* fell away second, after helping the spacecraft rise even higher.

f ....
This was the first stage of the rocket to fall away, after pushing the spacecraft 42 miles (68 km) high.

FILL IT IN!

THE APOLLO PROGRAM

In the 1960s, NASA began the Apollo Program—an ambitious mission aiming to land astronauts on the Moon. After a number of test flights and practice missions, the *Apollo 11* lunar module landed on the Moon on July 20, 1969. Its occupants, Neil Armstrong and Buzz Aldrin, became the first people ever to visit the Moon's surface.

BREAK THE NEWS

The news that the mission to the Moon had been successful and human beings had walked on its surface made news around the world. Fill in the blanks on this newspaper to tell the story of the first Moon landing.

=== **WORLD ★ NEWS** ===

MOON LANDING SUCCESS!

Today, July 20, _ _ _ _ , a craft has landed on the Moon. The *Apollo* _ _ mission was launched from Earth on July 16 aboard the _ _ _ _ _ _ _ _ rocket. Astronauts _ _ _ _ _ _ _ _ _ _ and _ _ _ _ _ _ _ _ _ _ _ _ _ _ _ _ climbed out of the _ _ _ _ _ _ _ _ _ _ _ _ to take humankind's first steps on the surface of our planet's only satellite, the Moon.

WHAT CAME HOME?

There was no part of the *Apollo 11* spacecraft that made the entire journey to the Moon's surface and back. Use the coloring key to see which parts of the spacecraft and *Saturn V* rocket were present for which parts of the journey.

Coloring key

- Saturn V
- Command module
- Service module
- Lunar module

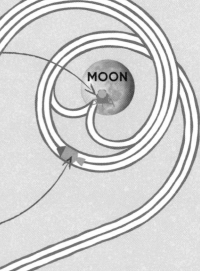

Third stage
The third stage rockets, which had blasted *Apollo 11* into space, continue on past the Moon.

MOON

Moon landing
The lunar module lands on the Moon, then rejoins the other modules.

Orbiting the Moon
The command and service modules continue around the Moon.

End of the road
The command module returns to Earth with the astronauts inside.

THE APOLLO 11 MISSION LASTED
8 DAYS, 3 HOURS, 18 MINUTES, AND 35 SECONDS.

COLOR IT!

EARTH

First and second stages
Two minutes and forty-two seconds after liftoff, the first stage of the *Saturn V* rocket falls away. After nine minutes and nine seconds, the second stage falls away. Both stages fall into the Atlantic Ocean.

FIND THE LANDING SITES

All of the Apollo missions landed toward the middle of the near side of the Moon. Use the coordinates given in the key below to help you plot each of them in the right place.

Key

- ✗ Apollo 15 (F,6)
- ✗ Apollo 17 (F,4)
- ✗ Apollo 11 (E,3)
- ✗ Apollo 12 (C,5)
- ✗ Apollo 16 (D,2)
- ✗ Apollo 14 (D,5)

WALKING ON THE MOON

Six *Apollo* modules landed on the Moon's surface between 1969 and 1972. Each of them carried two astronauts, who spent their time on the Moon collecting rock samples and exploring the lunar surface.

HOW HIGH?

Gravity on the Moon is not as strong as gravity on Earth. In fact, it is only one-sixth as strong, which means astronauts can jump six times higher than they could on Earth. This astronaut can jump 1.5 feet (0.5 m) on Earth. Use the grid below to draw him at the height he can jump on the Moon.

16.5 FEET (5 M)

13 FEET (4 M)

10 FEET (3 M)

6.5 FEET (2 M)

3 FEET (1 M)

DRAW IT!

96 BAGS OF URINE AND **FECES** HAVE BEEN LEFT ON **THE MOON.**

START HERE!

DRIVE THE LUNAR ROVER!

Steer the lunar rover through this maze back to the lunar module, making sure to collect all the rocks on your way.

FINISH HERE!

Lunar lander

The astronauts descended to the Moon in a lunar module. This tiny craft had two parts. The descent stage powered the descent to the Moon, then stayed there, becoming a launch pad. Only the ascent stage returned into orbit, using the descent stage to launch it.

Wide footpads were designed to stop the module from sinking into the ground.

COLOR THE LANDER

Using the image to the left as a guide, color in this scene showing the lunar lander and two astronauts on the Moon.

Radar antenna

Hatch to *Apollo* spacecraft

COLOR IT!

Thruster jets controlled the flight of the ascent stage.

Foil layers protected the craft from extreme temperatures.

Ladder

WHAT DID YOU COLLECT?

When you completed the maze on the left-hand page, you passed three things left behind by astronauts and lots of rocks. Draw what you spotted into these photo frames.

How many rocks did you collect on the way?

DRAW IT!

a ......
There is no wind on the Moon, so you can still see where astronauts have walked.

b ......
American astronauts have landed on the Moon six times and left this national symbol.

c ......
Astronauts have to carry out repairs, but tools are heavy, so they get left behind.

ON BOARD THE ISS

A space station is a permanent outpost that orbits the Earth in space. Space stations allow astronauts to live away from Earth for long periods of time and to conduct scientific research, such as experiments about zero gravity and conditions in space.

BUILD THE ISS

The International Space Station (ISS) was built in sections called modules. Each module was built on Earth, then joined to others in space. Use the key to help you color in this diagram of some of the modules. When complete, it will show you which space agency built each module.

Coloring key

1 NASA (the United States space agency)

2 Roscosmos (the Russian space agency)

3 JAXA (the Japanese space agency)

4 ESA (the European space agency)

5 CSA (the Canadian space agency)

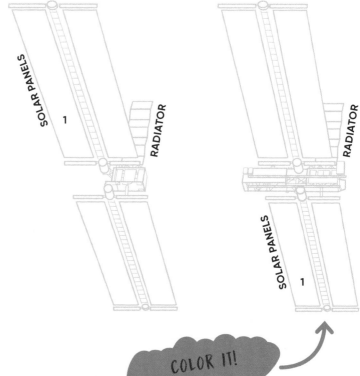

SOLAR PANELS

RADIATOR

1

RADIATOR

SOLAR PANELS

1

COLOR IT!

The International Space Station

The ISS is the largest space station ever built. It is powered by huge solar panels, which turn sunlight into electricity. There are several science laboratories and enough space for up to seven astronauts to live, work, and sleep.

WALK IN SPACE

Astronauts don't spend all their time inside the ISS. They sometimes need to go outside to maintain the station or add new parts. The official name for this is an "extravehicular activity" (EVA). Unscramble the letters below to reveal the less formal name for this activity.

P E C S A A L W K

_ _ _ _ _ _ _ _ _

DISCOVER A DAY IN THEIR LIFE

Gravity can hardly be felt on board the ISS. The people and objects float around, making everyday tasks tricky. Check the diary entries below that are true.

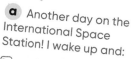
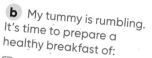

a Another day on the International Space Station! I wake up and:

☐ unzip my vertical sleeping bag
☐ climb out of my hammock

b My tummy is rumbling. It's time to prepare a healthy breakfast of:

☐ a packet of dried food mixed with water
☐ boiled noodles and vegetables

c Floating around means my bones and muscles may become weak, so I:

☐ run on the treadmill
☐ play badminton

d In microgravity, water floats away and gets into the electrics. So I wash by:

☐ squeezing rinseless soap onto my skin and hair
☐ taking a shower

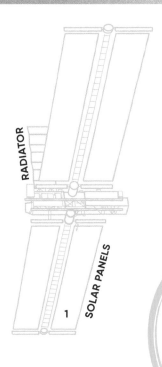

SERVICE MODULE 2

CARGO BLOCK 2

MOBILE SERVICING SYSTEM 1

4

RADIATOR

SOLAR PANELS 1

RADIATOR

SOLAR PANELS 1

LABORATORY 1

PRESSURIZED MODULE 3

5

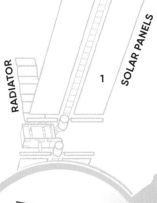

THE ISS ORBITS EARTH ABOUT 16 TIMES EVERY 24 HOURS.

SEARCHING FOR LIFE

So far, Earth is the only place in the universe known to support life. But are we really the only life in the universe? Some scientists have dedicated their careers to finding out. So far, more than 50 planets have been discovered in areas that are likely to be habitable.

Alien hunters

The organization SETI (which stands for the Search for Extraterrestrial Intelligence) began as part of NASA. Its scientists search the universe for signs of extraterrestrial intelligence. They even send messages into space using radio waves and listen for any replies.

PROJECT "BREAKTHROUGH LISTEN" HAS BEEN SCANNING **1 MILLION** STARS AND 100 GALACTIC CENTERS FOR LIFE SINCE 2016.

SEND A MESSAGE

In 1974, SETI scientists used the massive Arecibo Radio Telescope to send a message about life on our planet into space. Color the image to show different parts of this message.

Coloring key

1 2 3 4
5 6 7

COLOR IT!

The numbers 1 to 10, written in binary code

The chemical elements hydrogen, carbon, nitrogen, oxygen, and phosphorus, which are important for life on Earth

The key molecules that make up DNA

The twisted shape of DNA

A human and the population of Earth, in binary code

Our Solar System, with Earth lifted to highlight it

The Arecibo Radio Telescope, including radio waves

a ....

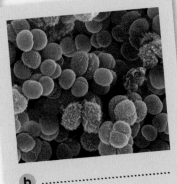

b ....

CAN YOU PICTURE AN ALIEN?

If there is life beyond our planet, it might look like one of these living things. Match the pictures to the descriptions. You'll need to draw one yourself!

LABEL IT!

DRAW IT!

Tardigrade
Tardigrades are tiny animals that can live under great pressure at the bottom of the ocean in very dry conditions or in extreme cold or heat.

Alien
Our bodies are shaped by the gravity, oxygen levels, and environment of planet Earth. Imagine a being from a very different planet and draw it in the box. Does it live on a hot planet or a cold one? How does it see, breathe, and touch?

Bacteria
Scientists believe that bacteria could survive underground on planets with harsh conditions. Some bacteria can resist heat, cold, and even intense radiation from the Sun.

My name is:

c ....

START HERE!

FIND THE ELEMENTS

Five chemical elements are needed to build human life. Trace a path through the grid to collect all five elements. Check the Arecibo message for a clue to the five elements you are looking for!

FINISH HERE!

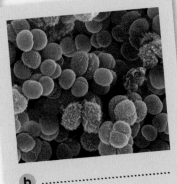

H Y S G E N
K D B O R T
O L U S N I U B U
G Q R O H P S Q S
R A C N E K I K Y G O F A
B O N O X Y G E N P H C H

STARS AND PLANETS QUIZ

Now it's time to test how much you've learned about stars and planets by taking this quiz. You can go back through earlier pages to look for clues and check up on some of the facts, if you need to. Good luck!

1 What is the name of our local star?

2 How many planets are there in the Solar System?

....

3 Which planet is closest to the Sun?

....

4 Earth is the only planet known to have which substance permanently present on its surface?

a Liquid nitrogen
b Solid mercury
c Liquid water
d Oxygen gas

5 Which of the following options is not a type of eclipse?

a Lunar
b Solar
c Martian
d Molar

6 Which was the first spacecraft to observe Neptune?

a *Voyager 2*
b *Voyager 1*
c *Cassini-Huygens*
d *Apollo*

7 Name the phenomenon shown in this photo.

....

8 How many meteorites hit Earth's surface each year?

- **a** Around 6,000
- **b** Less than 10
- **c** None
- **d** More than 8,000

9 From Earth, we always see the same side of the Moon.

☐ True ☐ False

10 Which of these planets is Mars?

a  ☐

b ☐

c 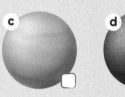 ☐

d ☐

11 Which of these is not a galaxy type?

- **a** Spiral
- **b** Shared Spiral
- **c** Elliptical
- **d** Irregular

12 Which was the only part of the *Apollo* spacecraft to make the journey back to Earth?

- **a** *Saturn V*
- **b** The command module
- **c** The lunar module
- **d** The service module

13 What was the name of the first satellite that was sent into space?

- **a** *Ariel*
- **b** *Sputnik*
- **c** *Echo*
- **d** *Swift*

14 What is the name of the largest space station ever built?

- **a** The National Martian
- **b** The Universal Space Box
- **c** The Global Station Exit
- **d** The International Space Station

15 Which tiny animal (pictured here) could survive in space?

....

16 Name these four giant planets.

a

....

b

....

c

....

d

....

SPACESCAPE!

It's a fine day on Mars, with views over our Solar System. Look carefully and you'll see our Sun, all eight planets, a comet, some asteroids, a rocket leaving Earth, and so much more. Color in the picture, then find and draw the items in the panel on the right.

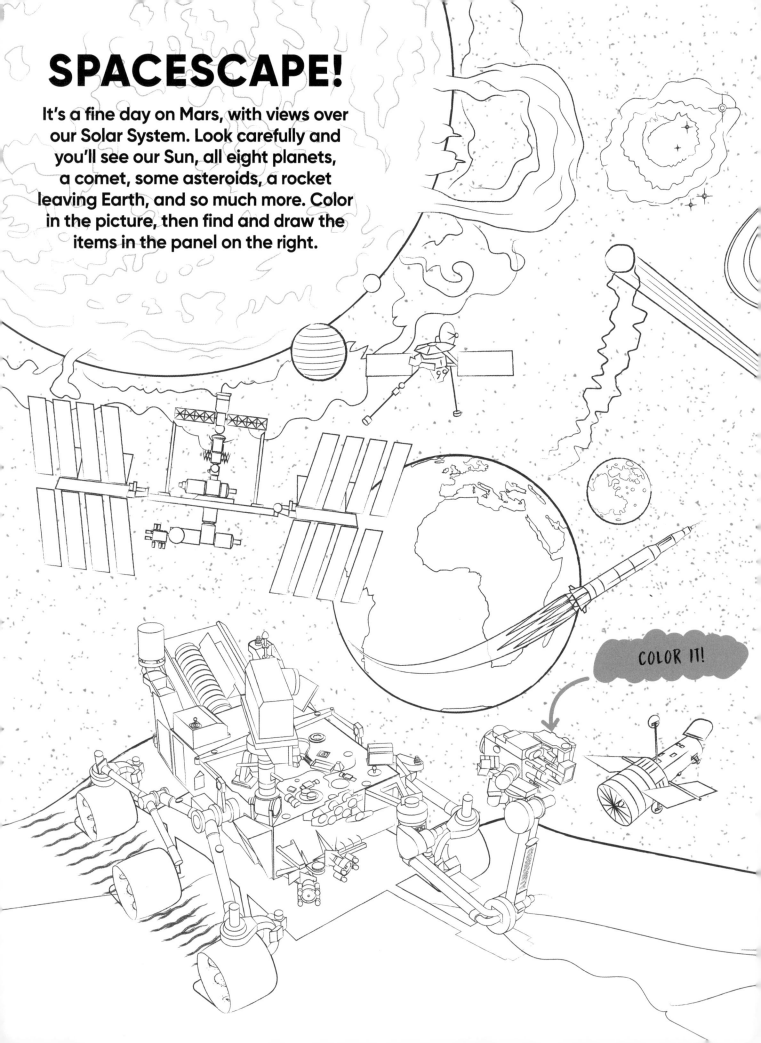

COLOR IT!

WHAT DO YOU SEE?

Find the five things listed below and draw them in the boxes.

DRAW IT!

Hubble Space Telescope

A nebula

International Space Station

A solar flare

A Mars rover

AMAZING SPACE

Our universe is home to stars, planets, and all sorts of other incredible phenomena. Here are just a few amazing facts about them.

Our Solar System

What exactly is in our Solar System? Here's what we know (at this moment in time) in numbers:

NUMBER OF STARS

JUST ONE

NUMBER OF DWARF PLANETS

5

NUMBER OF PLANETS

8

NUMBER OF PLANETARY MOONS

AROUND 185

NUMBER OF KNOWN COMETS

AROUND 4,584

NUMBER OF ASTEROIDS

MORE THAN 1 MILLION

Light distances

Light travels at 186,282 miles (299,792 km) per second. Here's how long it takes light to reach some places across the universe.

Sun to Earth:
8.3 minutes

Sun to Neptune:
2.7 hours

Sun to nearest star:
4.24 years

Sun to nearest galaxy outside the Milky Way, Canis Major Dwarf Galaxy:
25,000 years

Sun to farthest away object ever spotted, the HD1 galaxy:
13.5 billion light-years

Edge of the observable universe:
46.5 billion light-years

Winners

These planets and other space objects are all outstanding in their fields. Read on to find out why.

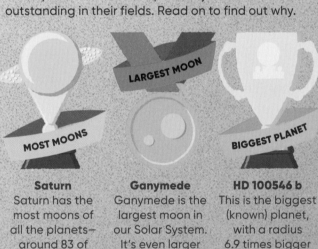

MOST MOONS · LARGEST MOON · BIGGEST PLANET

Saturn
Saturn has the most moons of all the planets—around 83 of them.

Ganymede
Ganymede is the largest moon in our Solar System. It's even larger than Mercury.

HD 100546 b
This is the biggest (known) planet, with a radius 6.9 times bigger than Jupiter's.

BIGGEST NEBULA · BIGGEST GALAXY · BIGGEST OBJECT

Tarantula
One of many giant nebulas, Tarantula is 1,862 light-years wide.

Galaxy IC 1101
This is the biggest known galaxy. It is 50 times bigger than our galaxy, the Milky Way.

The Sun
The Sun is the biggest object in our Solar System and makes up 99.8% of its mass.

Journeys around the Sun

Each planet in our Solar System takes a different amount of time to orbit the Sun, which equals the length of its year. The planets closest to the Sun orbit it most quickly, and those farther away more slowly.

Mercury
This planet orbits the Sun in the fastest time.

Earth
Every four years, an extra day is added to our year (a "leap year").

Jupiter
This spins fast on its own axis, so it has short, 10-hour days.

Uranus
Like Venus, it rotates in the opposite direction to the other planets.

PLANET

 88 DAYS

 **225 DAYS**

 365 DAYS

 687 DAYS

 694 DAYS

10,731 DAYS

 30,660 DAYS

60,225 DAYS

Venus
This is the hottest planet in the Solar System.

Mars
This is the most explored planet after Earth.

Saturn
It also has a 10-hour day, but its year lasts 29 Earth years!

Neptune
This faraway planet's year is 165 Earth years long.

Astronaut training

Becoming an astronaut takes years of hard work. Here are some of the things potential astronauts do to prepare them to journey into space:

Virtual reality
Because they have to train on Earth, astronauts practice in a virtual-reality environment.

Vomit Comet
Trainees float in the air in a reduced-gravity aircraft known as the "Vomit Comet."

Wear a spacesuit
Astronauts wear spacesuits underwater because it feels similar to being in zero gravity.

Centrifuge
Sitting in a centrifuge that spins very fast recreates the experience of liftoff and returning to Earth.

Suit fitting
Spacesuits are made in sections. Astronauts are measured carefully so their suit fits perfectly.

Getting ready
Astronauts train for two years in lots of subjects, from robotics and swimming to foreign languages.

GLOSSARY

Altimeter
An instrument that measures how high something is above the ground.

Asteroid
A small, irregular Solar System object made of rock and/or metal, which orbits the Sun.

Asteroid Belt
A donut-shaped region of the Solar System between the orbits of Mars and Jupiter, which contains a large number of orbiting asteroids.

Astronaut
A person trained to travel and live in space. Russian astronauts are known as cosmonauts.

Astronomical unit (AU)
The average distance between Earth and the Sun, equal to 93 million miles (150 million km).

Astronomy
The science of planets, stars, and other celestial bodies.

Atmosphere
The layer of gas that surrounds a planet. Also the outermost layer of gas around the Sun or a star.

Atom
The smallest particle of a chemical element that can exist on its own.

Aurora
Patterns of light that appear near the poles of some planets.

Axis
An imaginary line that passes through the center of a star or planet, and around which it rotates.

Big Bang
The way the universe began—a sudden burst of matter and energy.

Binary star
A pair of stars that orbit around each other.

Black hole
An object in space with such a strong gravitational pull that nothing can escape it, not even light.

Celestial
In or relating to the sky or outer space.

Comet
An object made of dust and ice that travels around the Sun in an elliptical orbit.

Constellation
A group of stars that form a pattern and have a name.

Core
The hot center of a planet or star.

Cosmonaut
See "astronaut."

Crater
A bowl- or saucer-shaped depression on the surface of a planet, moon, or asteroid, created by something hitting it or by a volcano.

Crewed
Containing a crew of people.

Crust
The thin, solid outer layer of a planet or moon.

Debris
Material left behind after a star or planet has formed or been destroyed.

Deflect
To make something change direction.

Density
The amount of matter that occupies a certain volume.

Detect
To find or discover.

Diameter
The distance through the center of a circle or sphere, from one side to the opposite side.

Dock
When a craft comes alongside and joins onto another.

Dwarf planet
A planet that is big enough to have become spherical but hasn't cleared its orbital path.

Eclipse
When an object crosses the shadow of another object or temporarily blocks an observer's view.

Equator
An imaginary line around the center of a planet, halfway between its north and south poles.

EVA
Extravehicular activity—activity undertaken by an astronaut in outer space, outside a spacecraft.

Exoplanet
A planet that orbits a star other than the Sun.

Extraterrestrial
Of or from outside Earth.

Fusion
A process whereby atomic nuclei join together to form heavier nuclei, releasing huge amounts of energy.

Galaxy
A collection of millions or trillions of stars, gas, and dust held together by gravity.

Gas giant
A huge planet made of gas.

Geyser
A hot spring that spurts a column of water and steam into the air.

Gravity
The force that pulls all objects toward one another.

Habitable
Suitable for living in or on.

Hemisphere
One half of a sphere. Earth is divided into northern and southern hemispheres by its equator.

Horizontal
Parallel to the horizon.

Ice giant
A huge planet made of a mixture of gas and icy materials.

Impact
When one object hits another.

Interstellar
Between the stars.

ISS
The International Space Station.

Light-year
The distance that light travels in one year.

Lunar
Relating to the Moon.

Magnetic field
An area around a magnetic object (like most stars and planets), which pulls on metal objects.

Main-sequence star
An ordinary star, such as our Sun, which shines by converting hydrogen to helium.

Mantle
A thick layer of hot rock between the core and the crust of a planet or moon.

Martian
Relating to the planet Mars.

Mass
The amount of matter that an object contains.

Meteor
A streak of light seen when a meteoroid burns up on entering Earth's atmosphere. Also called a shooting star.

Methane
A colorless, odorless gas.

Molten
Made liquid by heat.

Moon
A natural satellite orbiting around a planet or other object.

NASA
The National Aeronautics and Space Administration—the United States' space agency.

Nebula
A cloud of gas and/or dust in space.

Nucleus
The compact central core of an atom. Also the solid, icy body of a comet.

Orbit
The curved path taken by one object around another in space.

Orbiter
A spacecraft that is designed to orbit an object but not land on it.

Particle
An extremely small part of a solid, liquid, or gas.

Plane
A flat, two-dimensional surface.

Planet
A spherical object that orbits a star and is sufficiently massive to have cleared its orbital path of debris.

Plasma
A highly energized form of gas in which the atoms have broken apart.

Probe
An uncrewed spacecraft that is designed to explore objects in space and transmit information back to Earth.

Quintillion
A billion billions.

Radiation
Waves of energy that travel through space.

Red giant
A large, luminous star with a low surface temperature and a reddish color. It "burns" helium in its core instead of hydrogen and is nearing the final stages of its life.

Rocky planet
A planet that is small and rocky, with a solid surface, sometimes with oceans.

Rover
A vehicle that is driven remotely on the surface of a planet or moon.

Satellite
An object that orbits another object larger than itself. Either a moon or a spacecraft put into orbit.

Solar
Relating to the Sun.

Solar flare
A brief release of huge amounts of electromagnetic energy from the Sun's surface.

Solar System
Our Sun together with the objects that orbit it.

Solar wind
A continuous flow of fast-moving charged particles from the Sun.

Sphere
A 3D shape that is round like a ball.

Spherical
Shaped like a sphere.

Star
A huge sphere of glowing plasma that generates energy by nuclear fusion in its core.

Universe
Everything in space, including all the stars, nebulas, and galaxies.

ANSWERS

4-5 **WHERE ARE WE?**

COMPLETE THE SET

a Earth
The planet we live on

b Solar System
The Sun and the group of planets that orbit it

c Milky Way
A galaxy that contains many stars, including the Sun

d Universe
A vast expanse that contains everything there is

FIND THE WORDS

DRAW THE UNIVERSE

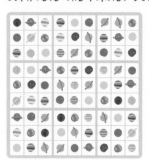

6-7 **OUR SOLAR SYSTEM**

COMPLETE THE PLANET-DOKU

BONUS QUESTION
Solar

WHICH PLANET IS WHICH?

a Mars
b Uranus
c Saturn
d Earth
e Mercury
f Jupiter
g Neptune
h Venus

8-9 **THE SUN**

LABEL A SUNSPOT

a Photosphere
b Penumbra
c Umbra

SHADE THE LAYERS

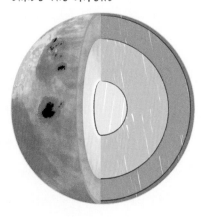

MATCH THE STEPS

1 b
2 c
3 a

COMPLETE THE WORD SNAKE

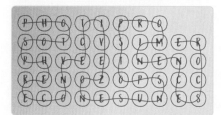

10-11 **AURORAS**

WHICH SHAPE?

a Crown
b Curtain
c Bands

FIND THE AURORAS
Aurora borealis at the North Pole
Aurora australis at the South Pole

DESIGN AN AURORA
Here's what ours looks like!

12-13 **ROCKY PLANETS AND GIANT PLANETS**

WHICH IS WHICH?
Mercury—rocky planet
Saturn—giant planet
Earth—rocky planet
Neptune—giant planet

UNSCRAMBLE THE NAME
Atmosphere

SPLIT THEM UP

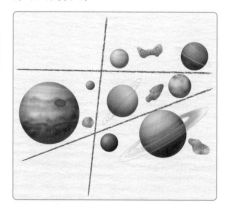

14-15 MERCURY

MATCH THE FEATURES
a Caloris Basin
b Kuiper Crater
c Plains

COMPLETE THE MISSIONS
Mariner 10
Took the first photos of Mercury's surface

BepiColombo
To send two spacecrafts together to Mercury

Messenger
2004

COLOR THE MAP

16-17 VENUS

TWIN PLANETS?
Earth
Atmosphere: Mostly nitrogen and oxygen
Surface temperature: 60°F (15°C)
Life: Plants and animals

Venus
Atmosphere: Mostly carbon dioxide
Surface temperature: 900°F (475°C)
Life: No life

WHERE IS VENUS?
5

WHY SO HOT?

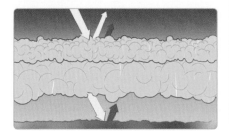

18-19 EARTH

WHERE IS IT JUST RIGHT?

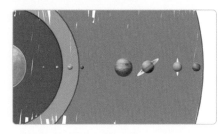

WHAT HAPPENS WHERE?

 Exosphere

 Thermosphere

 Mesosphere

 Stratosphere

 Troposphere

20-21 OUR MOON

MATCH THE LUNAR CRATERS
1 b
2 d
3 a
4 c

WHICH SIDE?
a Nearside
b Farside

COMPLETE THE PHASES

New Moon   Waxing crescent

First quarter   Waxing gibbous

Full Moon   Wanning gibbous

Last quarter   Waning crescent

22-23 ECLIPSES

FINISH THE ECLIPSE

BONUS QUESTION
Annular solar eclipse

NAME THAT SHADOW
Penumbra

WHICH EFFECT IS WHICH?
a Baily's beads
b Annular solar eclipse
c Sun's corona
d Partial solar eclipse
e Diamond ring effect

24-25 MARS

COLOR THE PLANET

NAME THE MOONS

- **a** Phobos
- **b** Deimos

LOCATE THE LIQUID WATER

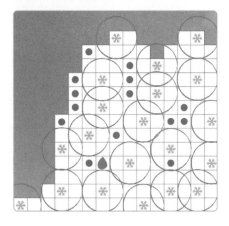

26-27 ASTEROIDS

FIND THE ASTEROIDS

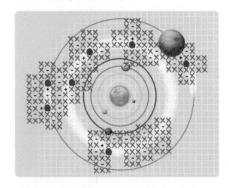

WHICH IS WHICH?

- **a** Toutatis
- **b** Kleopatra
- **c** Ceres
- **d** Ida

COLOR THE ORBITS

28-29 JUPITER

JUST HOW BIG IS JUPITER?

▲ 80
● 5

$$80 \div 5 - 5 = 11$$

FIND THE WORDS

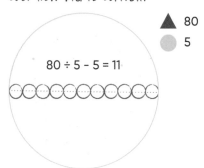

30-31 SATURN

COMPLETE THE RINGS

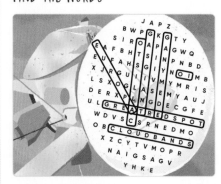

REVEAL THE MOON
Titan

DESIGN A RING SYSTEM
Here's what our planet looks like!

32-33 URANUS

TILT THE PLANET

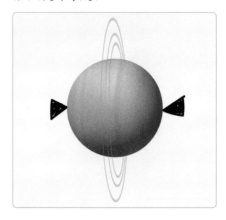

COMPLETE THE CRYSTAL

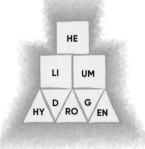

WHICH MOON IS WHICH?

- **a** Puck
- **b** Miranda
- **c** Ariel
- **d** Umbriel
- **e** Oberon
- **f** Titania

34-35 NEPTUNE

COMPLETE THE TIMELINE
1979—Jupiter
1981—Saturn
1986—Uranus
1989—Neptune

VOYAGER'S VOYAGE?
The blue route

SPOT THE STORM

36-37 DWARF PLANETS

HOW BIG IS PLUTO?
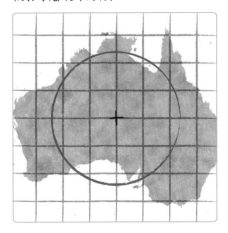

BONUS QUESTION
The Kuiper Belt

WHAT IS IT?
- **a** Asteroid
- **b** Moon
- **c** Planet
- **d** Dwarf planet

SORT THE DWARF PLANETS
- **a** Haumea
- **b** Eris
- **c** Pluto
- **d** Makemake
- **e** Ceres

38-39 COMETS

COLOR THE TAILS

WHAT YEARS?
1607, 1682, 1758

SPOT THE IMPOSTOR
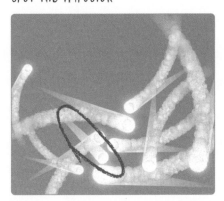

FIND THE NAME
Coma

40-41 METEORITES

MATCH THE METEORITES
- **a** Stony
- **b** Stony-iron
- **c** Iron

REARRANGE IT
Crater

NAME THAT ROCK
- **a** Asteroid
- **b** Meteoroid
- **c** Meteor
- **d** Meteorite

DRAW A METEOR SHOWER
Here's what ours looks like!

42-43 STARS

HOW HOT ARE THEY?

FIND THE STARS
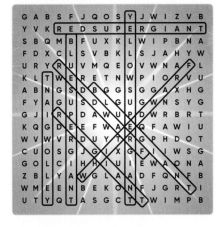

FILL IN THE MISSING FACTS
Proxima centauri
Orange-red
4.4 light-years

Betelgeuse
Red supergiant

Sirius A
White main-sequence star
1.7 times the Sun's diameter

44-45 LIFE CYCLE OF A STAR

DRAW THE STAR MEMORIES

a
Nebula

b
Main sequence

c
Red supergiant

d
Supernova

e
Neutron star

WHAT'S IT CALLED?
Black hole

FIND THE BALANCE

 a Red giant

 b Black hole

 c Normal star

46-47 EXOPLANETS

FIND A NEW HOME
Planet D

SORT THE SYSTEMS
GJ 357—Super-Earth

Kepler-47—Pair of stars

Kepler-62—Sun-like

PUT A PLANET IN ITS BOX
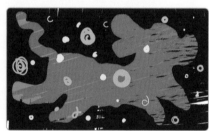

48-49 NEBULAS

WHAT CAN YOU SEE?
a Close-up

b Naked eye

c Zooming in

QUIZ YOURSELF!
a Emission nebula

b False (they are usually blue)

c Supernova remnants

d Dark nebula

e Planetary nebula

CREATE YOUR OWN NEBULA
Here's what ours looks like!
We named it Puppy Nebula.

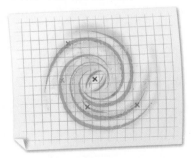

50-51 GALAXIES

CROSS THE CLUSTER GALAXY
It took us 16 million light-years.

WHICH SHAPE IS WHICH?
a Irregular

b Elliptical

c Barred spiral

d Spiral

SOLVE THE GALAXY-DOKU

REVEAL THE GALAXY

BONUS QUESTION
Barred spiral

52-53 THE MILKY WAY

NAME THAT ARM!
a Orion Arm

b Perseus Arm

c Norma Arm

d Sagittarius Arm

LABEL THE GALAXY
a Main disk

b Central bulge

BUILD THE MILKY WAY

DRAW THE VIEW
Here's what ours looks like!

54-55 LOOKING UP

COLOR THE SPHERES

View from the North Pole

View from the midlatitudes

View from the equator

WHAT CAN YOU SEE?
a The Sun
b The Milky Way
c The Moon
d A meteor
e The constellation Orion

NAME THE SYSTEM
a Heliocentric
b Geocentric

56-57 CONSTELLATIONS

MATCH THE STORIES
a Leo
b Centaurus
c Orion
d Cygnus

DESIGN YOUR OWN CONSTELLATIONS
Here's what ours looks like!

HOW FAR?

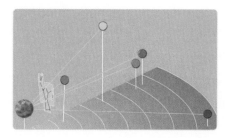

58-59 STAR MAPS

COMPLETE THE CONSTELLATIONS

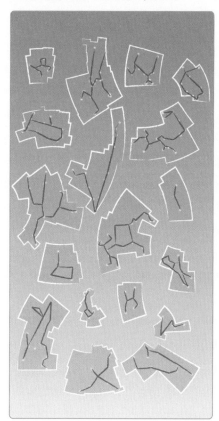

60-61 TELESCOPES

REFLECT OR REFRACT?

a Refracting   b Reflecting

WHAT CAN YOU SEE?

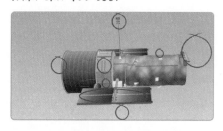

COMPLETE THE FACT FILES
Very large telescope
27 feet (8.2 m)

Keck telescopes
Mauna Kea, Hawaii

Gran Telescopio Canarias
7,440 feet (2,267 m)

62-63 SPACE EXPLORATION

WHO WENT FIRST?
Yuri Gagarin

WHAT HAPPENED WHEN?
a 1957
b 1961
c 1963
d 1969
e 1998

MATCH THE ANIMALS
a Ham
b Tardigrades
c Belka and Strelka

DESIGN A MARS SPACESUIT
Here's what ours looks like!

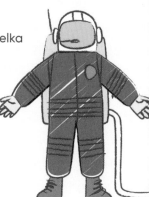

COMPLETE THE ROCKET

a Thrust
b Liquid oxygen
c Fuel
d Combustion chamber
e Nozzle
f Hot exhaust gases

MATCH THE STAGES
From top to bottom: 4, 2, 1, 5, 3

FIND THE NAME
Liftoff

ENOUGH THRUST?

a ▲   b ▼   c ▼
d ▼   e ▲

PROBE THE SOLAR SYSTEM

a *Magellan*
b *Mars Reconnaissance Orbiter*
c *Parker Solar Probe*
d *Cassini-Huygens*
e *Pioneer 10*

MATCH AND IDENTIFY

a *New Horizons*, flyby
b *Juno*, orbiter
c *OSIRIS-REx*, lander
d *Opportunity*, rover

MARTIAN VIEWS

a *Opportunity*
b *Sojourner*
c *Curiosity*
d *Perseverance*

COMPLETE THE FACT FILES

Sojourner
Weight of rover: 25.4 lb (11.5 kg)
Date launched: December 4, 1996

Curiosity
Agency: NASA
Landing site: Gale Crater

Zhurong
Date launched: July 23, 2020
Date of arrival: May 14, 2021

DESIGN YOUR OWN ROVER
Here's what ours looks like!

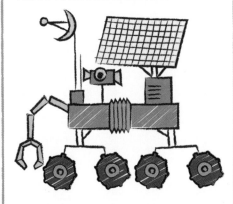

JOURNEY INTO SPACE AND BACK

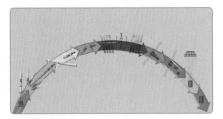

WHICH CRAFT IS WHICH?

Space shuttle

SpaceX *Crew Dragon*

SpaceShipTwo

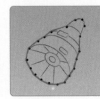
Gemini

LABEL THE SPACECRAFT

a Command module
b Service module
c Lunar module
d Third stage
e Second stage
f First stage

BREAK THE NEWS
1969, 11, *Saturn V*, Neil Armstrong, Buzz Aldrin, lunar module

WHAT CAME HOME?

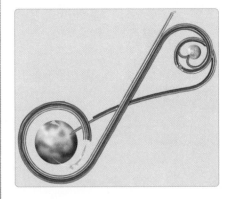

FIND THE LANDING SITES

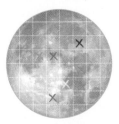

HOW HIGH?

DRIVE THE LUNAR ROVER!

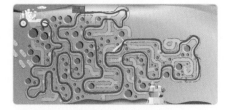

COLOR THE LANDER

WHAT DID YOU COLLECT?

14 rocks and these three objects:

a

b

Footprint

Flag

c

Hammer

76-77 **ON BOARD THE ISS**

BUILD THE ISS

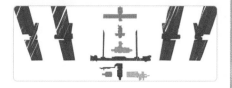

WALK IN SPACE

Spacewalk

DISCOVER A DAY IN THEIR LIFE

a Unzip my vertical sleeping bag

b A packet of dried food mixed with water

c Run on the treadmill

d Squeezing rinseless soap onto my skin and hair

78-79 **SEARCHING FOR LIFE**

SEND A MESSAGE

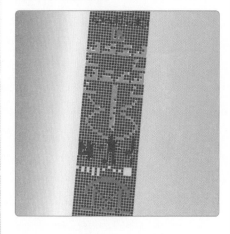

CAN YOU PICTURE AN ALIEN?

a Tardigrade

b Bacteria

c Alien

Here's what our alien looks like!

FIND THE ELEMENTS

Hydrogen, Carbon, Oxygen, Phosphorus, Nitrogen

80-81 **STARS AND PLANETS QUIZ**

1 The Sun
2 8
3 Mercury
4 c. Liquid water
5 d. Molar
6 a. *Voyager 2*
7 Aurora
8 a. Around 6,000
9 True
10 d.
11 b. Shared Spiral
12 b. The command module
13 b. *Sputnik*
14 d. The International Space Station
15 Tardigrade
16 a. Jupiter, b. Saturn, c. Uranus, d. Neptune

82-83 **SPACESCAPE!**

DRAW YOUR OWN!

Here's what ours looks like!

INDEX

ACKNOWLEDGMENTS

DK would like to thank the following for their help with this book: John Friend for proofreading; Elizabeth Wise for compiling the index; Andrea Page for editorial assistance; Mark Ruffle for illustrating the answers; and Laura Gardner for additional jacket design.

The publisher would like to thank the following for their kind permission to reproduce their photographs:

(Key: a-above; b-below/bottom; c-center; f-far; l-left; r-right; t-top)

9 NASA: SDO (tr). 10 Alamy Stock Photo: mauritius images GmbH / Arctic-Images (c); Alan Dyer / Stocktrek Images (cr). Getty Images / iStock: Biletskiy_Evgeniy (fcr). 13 NASA: (tr). 14 NASA: Johns Hopkins University Applied Physics Laboratory / Carnegie Institution of Washington (clb, cb); Johns Hopkins University Applied Physics Laboratory / Arizona State University / Carnegie Institution of Washington. Image reproduced courtesy of Science / AAAS. (fclb). 14-15 NASA: Johns Hopkins University Applied Physics Laboratory / Carnegie Institution of Washington (t). 15 NASA: (clb, crb). Science Photo Library: European Space Agency (cb). 20 NASA: Goddard / Lunar Reconnaissance Orbiter (b). 21 NASA: Goddard / Lunar Reconnaissance Orbiter (Phases). 25 NASA: (tc); JPL-Caltech / University of Arizona (tr). 28 Alamy Stock Photo: World History Archive (clb/X4). 35 NASA: (tr); JPL (cr). 36 NASA: Johns Hopkins University Applied Physics Laboratory / Southwest Research Institute (cb). 37 Alamy Stock Photo: MR3D (crb). NASA: Johns Hopkins University Applied Physics Laboratory / Southwest Research Institute (cb); JPL-Caltech / UCLA / MPS / DLR / IDA (crb/Ceres). Science Photo Library: Mark Garlick (clb/X2). 39 Science Photo Library: Dan Schechter (tr). 40 Dorling Kindersley: Colin Keates / Natural History Museum, London (cra). 41 Getty Images: Moment / Dneutral Han (br). 43 ESA / Hubble: NASA (clb). NASA: ESA, H. Bond (STScI) and M. Barstow (University of Leicester) (crb). Science Photo

Library: Alma (Eso / Naoj / Nrao) / E. Ogorman / P. Kervella / European Southern Observatory (cb). 48 Alamy Stock Photo: Roberto Colombari / Stocktrek Images (clb). NASA: ESA / JPL / Arizona State Univ. (bc); JPL-Caltech / STScI (cla); NOAO, ESA, the Hubble Helix Nebula Team, M. Meixner (STScI), and T. A. Rector (NRAO) (crb). Science Photo Library: Tony & Daphne Hallas (cra). 49 Dreamstime.com: Sdrart (cla). Getty Images / iStock: JULIAN74 (ca). NASA: ESA / Hubble (bl); JPL-Caltech / STScI (cla/Orion); ESA / STScI (bc). 50 Science Photo Library: NASA / ESA / STSCI / A.FRUCHTER, ERO TEAM (cra). 51 NASA: CXC / MSU / J. Strader et al., Optical: NASA / STScI (tc); ESA / Hubble (tl); CXC / SAO; Optical: Detlef Hartmann; Infrared: NASA / JPL-Caltech (ca). Science Photo Library: Mark Garlick (cla). 53 Alamy Stock Photo: Jamie Pham (tr). 55 Alamy Stock Photo: Jamie Pham (cra). Dreamstime.com: Antonio Corrado (ca/Moon); Brett Critchley (ca); Sdrart (cr). NASA: Goddard / Lunar Reconnaissance Orbiter (br). Shutterstock.com: Nazarii_Neshcherenskyi (cb). 56 Dreamstime.com: Yuriykulik (tr). 61 Alamy Stock Photo: BIOSPHOTO / Alberto Ghizzi Panizza (cl). Dreamstime.com: Valentin M Armianu (c). Getty Images: imageBROKER / Sonja Jordan (cr). 62 Alamy Stock Photo: Pictorial Press Ltd. (bc). NASA: (bl, br, br/Spacewalk). 63 Alamy Stock Photo: Fine Art Images / Heritage Images (clb); PictureLux / The Hollywood Archive (cl); Science Photo Library (c). 65 NASA: (cb). 67 NASA: (clb, crb/Rover); JPL-Caltech (cb); NASA's Goddard Space Flight Center (crb). 68 NASA: JPL-Caltech / MSSS (clb); JPL-Caltech / Cornell University (cb); JPL-Caltech / ASU (crb); JPL (crb/Twin Peaks). 69 Alamy Stock Photo: Geopix (ca). NASA: JPL (cla). Shutterstock.com: Raymond Cassel (cra). 71 NASA: Bill Ingalls (br). 72 NASA: (crb). 73 NASA: (bl); Goddard / Lunar Reconnaissance Orbiter (bc/tr). 77 NASA: (cra, cra/Paolo, cra/Karen, cra/Eating). 79 Alamy Stock Photo: Science Photo Library (tl). Science Photo Library: Dennis Kunkel Microscopy (tc). 80 Getty Images / iStock: Biletskiy_Evgeniy (br). 81 Alamy Stock Photo: Science Photo Library (bc).

All other images © Dorling Kindersley